SERMON
ON THE MOUNT

DEEPENING
LIFE
TOGETHER

SERMON
ON THE MOUNT

LIFETOGETHER

BakerBooks
a division of Baker Publishing Group
Grand Rapids, Michigan

Published by Baker Books
a division of Baker Publishing Group
P.O. Box 6287, Grand Rapids, MI 49516-6287
www.bakerbooks.com

Printed in the United States of America

Library of Congress Cataloging-in-Publication Data
Sermon on the mount.
      p.   cm. — (Deepening life together)
   Includes bibliographical references.
   ISBN 978-0-8010-6919-2 (pbk.)
   1. Sermon on the mount—Textbooks.
 BT380.3.S47 2011
 226.9′06—dc22   2011006251

11 12 13 14 15 16 17   7 6 5 4 3 2 1

CONTENTS

Contents

ACKNOWLEDGMENTS

The *Deepening Life Together: Sermon on the Mount* Small Group Video Bible Study has come together through the efforts of many at Baker Publishing Group, Lifetogether Publishing, and Lamplighter Media for which we express our heartfelt thanks.

Executive Producer	John Nill
Producer and Director	Sue Doc Ross
Editors	Mark L. Strauss (Scholar), Teresa Haymaker
Curriculum Development	Brett Eastman, Sue Doc Ross, Mark L. Strauss, Teresa Haymaker, Stephanie French, Karen Lee-Thorp
Video Production	Chris Balish, Rodney Bissell, Nick Calabrese, Sebastian Hoppe Fuentes, Josh Greene, Patrick Griffin, Teresa Haymaker, Oziel Jabin Ibarra, Natali Ibarra, Janae Janik, Keith Sorrell, Lance Tracy, Sophie Olson, Ian Ross
Teachers and Scholars	Greg Sidders, Mark Strauss, Scott Duvall, Erik Thoennes, Craig Keener, Gene Green, Nick Perrin, Jon Laansma
Baker Publishing Group	Jack Kuhatschek

Special thanks to: DeLisa Ivy, Bethel Seminary, Talbot School of Theology, Wheaton College

Clips from The JESUS Film are copyright © 1995–2010 The JESUS Film Project®. A ministry of Campus Crusade for Christ International®.

Interior icons by Tom Clark

READ ME FIRST

Welcome to the *Deepening Life Together* study on the *Sermon on the Mount*. For some of you, this might be the first time you've connected in a small group community. We want you to know that God cares about you and your spiritual growth. As you prayerfully respond to the principles you learn in this study, God will move you to a deeper level of commitment and intimacy with himself, as well as with those in your small group.

We at Baker Books and Lifetogether Publishing look forward to hearing the stories of how God changes you from the inside out during this small group experience. We pray God blesses you with all he has planned for you through this journey together.

> For the LORD is good and his love endures forever;
> his faithfulness continues through all generations.
>
> Psalm 100:5

Session Outline

Most people want to live a healthy, balanced spiritual life, but few achieve this by themselves. And most small groups struggle to balance all of God's purposes in their meetings. Groups tend to overemphasize one of the five purposes, perhaps fellowship or discipleship.

Rarely is there a healthy balance that includes evangelism, ministry, and worship. That's why we've included all of these elements in this study so you can live a healthy, balanced spiritual life over time.

A typical group session will include the following:

Memory Verses

For each session we have provided a Memory Verse that emphasizes an important truth from the session. This is an optional exercise, but we believe that memorizing Scripture can be a vital part of filling our minds with God's Word. We encourage you to give this important habit a try.

CONNECTING *with God's Family (Fellowship)*

The foundation for spiritual growth is an intimate connection with God and his family. A few people who really know you and who earn your trust provide a place to experience the life Jesus invites you to live. This section of each session typically offers you two activities.

You can get to know your whole group by using the icebreaker question, and/or you can check in with one or two group members— your spiritual partner(s)—for a deeper connection and encouragement in your spiritual journey.

DVD Teaching Segment

A *Deepening Life Together: Sermon on the Mount* Video Teaching DVD companion to this study guide is available. For each study session, the DVD contains a lesson taught by Greg Sidders. If you are using the DVD, you will view the teaching segment after your *Connecting* discussion and before your group discussion time (the *Growing* section).

GROWING *to Be Like Christ (Discipleship)*

Here is where you come face-to-face with Scripture. In core passages you'll explore what the Bible teaches about the topic of the study. The focus won't be on accumulating information but on how we should live in light of the Word of God. We want to help you apply the Scriptures practically, creatively, and from your heart as well as your head. At the end of the day, allowing the timeless truths from God's Word to transform our lives in Christ is our greatest aim.

DEVELOPING *Your Gifts to Serve Others (Ministry)*

Jesus trained his disciples to discover and develop their gifts to serve others. And God has designed each of us uniquely to serve him in a way no other person can. This section will help you discover and use your God-given design. It will also encourage your group to discover your unique design as a community. In this study, you'll put into practice what you've learned in the Bible study by taking a step to serve others. These simple steps will take your group on a faith journey that could change your lives forever.

SHARING *Your Life Mission Every Day (Evangelism)*

Many people skip over this aspect of the Christian life because it's scary, relationally awkward, or simply too much work for their busy schedules. But Jesus wanted all of his disciples to help outsiders connect with him, to know him personally. This doesn't mean preaching on street corners. It could mean welcoming a few newcomers into your group, hosting a short-term group in your home, or walking through this study with a friend. In this study, you'll have an opportunity to go beyond Bible study to biblical living.

SURRENDERING *Your Life for God's Pleasure (Worship)*

God is most pleased by a heart that is fully his. Each group session will give you a chance to surrender your heart to God in prayer and worship. You may read a psalm together, share a page in your journal, or sing a song to close your meeting. If you have never prayed aloud in a group before, no one will pressure you. Instead, you'll experience the support of others who are praying for you.

Study Notes

This section provides background notes on the Bible passage(s) you examine in the *Growing* section. You may want to refer to these notes during your group meeting or as a reference for those doing additional study.

For Deeper Study (optional)

Some sessions provide *For Deeper Study*. If you want to dig deeper into more Bible passages about the topic at hand, we've provided additional passages and questions. Your group may choose to do study homework ahead of each meeting in order to cover more biblical material. Or you as an individual may choose to study the *For Deeper Study* on your own. If you prefer not to do study homework, the *Growing* section will provide you with plenty to discuss within the group. These options allow individuals or the whole group to go deeper in their study, while still accommodating those who can't do homework or are new to your group. You can record your discoveries in your journal. We encourage you to read some of your insights to a friend (spiritual partner) for accountability and support. Spiritual partners may check in each week over the phone, through e-mail, or at the beginning of the group meeting.

Reflections

On the *Reflections* pages we provide Scriptures to read and reflect on between group meetings. We suggest you use this section to seek God at home throughout the week. This time at home should begin and end with prayer. Don't get in a hurry; take enough time to hear God's direction.

Subgroup for Discussion and Prayer

If your group is large (more than seven people), we encourage you to separate into groups of two to four for discussion and prayer. This is to encourage greater participation and deeper discussion.

INTRODUCTION

In 2004, a massive earthquake measuring over 9.0 on the Richter scale occurred under the Indian Ocean just off the Indonesian island of Sumatra. Within hours of the earthquake, 50-foot killer tsunami waves slammed into coastlines, snatching people out to sea, drowning others in their homes or on beaches, and demolishing property. The tsunamis generated by the earthquake killed over 150,000 people in 14 countries—Bangladesh, India, Indonesia, Kenya, Malaysia, Maldives, Myanmar, Seychelles, Somalia, South Africa, Sri Lanka, Tanzania, Thailand, and Yemen.

Tsunamis occur when violent movements of the Earth's undersea tectonic plates displace an enormous amount of water, sending powerful waves in every direction. The waves travel as fast as 450 miles per hour from the area of the disturbance, much like the ripples that happen after throwing a rock into a pool of water. As the large waves approach shallow waters along the coast, they grow to as high as 100 feet.

The West Coast of the United States gets damaging tsunamis about every 18 years. Hawaii experiences damage from tsunamis about every 7 years. To protect themselves and their homes from the massive destruction caused by tsunamis, the Tsunami Warning Centers in Honolulu, Hawaii, and Palmer, Alaska, were created to monitor disturbances that might trigger a tsunami. When a tsunami is detected, the center tracks it and issues warnings when needed.

Before this warning system was in place, many people lost their lives and/or livelihood to the devastating effects of the tsunami. Now, people in this region of the world have time to prepare and evacuate to safety.

Just as the tsunami warning system enables people to prepare for what is coming, John the Baptist came to prepare the hearts and minds of the people for what is to come for eternity—the kingdom of heaven. John prepared the way for Jesus Christ, in whom God came to earth and began the establishment of his kingdom on earth. Like the consequences of being unprepared for an approaching tsunami or other natural disaster, we will each face very serious consequences if we do not prepare ourselves for God's kingdom. The Bible tells us how to do this.

During the next six weeks, we will discover what it means to be members of the kingdom as we examine the powerful teaching Jesus delivered in the first of his great sermons—the Sermon on the Mount. In this sermon, Jesus establishes the way by which the citizens of God's kingdom shall live.

Jesus's teaching shows that God's standard for ethical living is so high that its demands can't be met without God working inside us, transforming and empowering us at the heart level. Unlike the Mosaic system of sacrifices for atonement of sin, which called for ritualistic conformity to the Law, Jesus calls for inward heart transformation. His teaching should not seem like a burden but should drive us to complete dependence upon God.

This sermon leaves no doubt in the minds of its hearers that salvation cannot be earned by human merit but is given freely through the bountiful divine grace of God upon hearts that are yielded fully to him. Once our hearts are yielded to him, we shall see the transformation of our outward behavior as well.

PEOPLE WHO CHANGE THE WORLD

MEMORY VERSE: Blessed are they whose ways are blameless, who walk according to the law of the LORD. Blessed are they who keep his statutes and seek him with all their heart (Ps. 119:1–2).

In 2004, James and his family seemed to have it all: a multimillion-dollar home with high-tech toys, a swimming pool, a tennis court, and a four-car garage filled with SUVs. James, a successful business-man, spent the previous four years building a lucrative computer business that supported over 285 employees.

After being featured on the cover of a popular international in-dustry magazine as the number one fastest growing firm, James became a target for greedy businessmen who coveted his success and acquired wealth. Consequently, the years that followed were riddled with false accusations, lawsuits, and anxiety. By 2006, James had lost it all—or so it seemed to the outside world.

To settle the lawsuits, James gave away the company, millions of dollars, and sold whatever toys that remained. For the first time he was poor. It was during a lunch meeting with two Christian busi-nessmen that James rededicated his life to the Lord.

Starting over, James began to build a consulting firm founded on biblical principles. His focus switched from acquiring wealth to building up people. Since then, James has successfully coached over 300 companies to grow their business with a variety of coaching programs through accountability, encouragement, and integrity. His guiding verse is Philippians 4:4: "Rejoice in the Lord always. I will say it again: Rejoice!"

During a recent national coaching seminar, James stated, "It was when I was content to give it all away that God truly enriched my life."

During this session we will discuss how the Beatitudes turn the world's values upside down. We will explore and understand how God truly wants to bless and enhance our lives, and how these blessings can help us become people who change the world.

CONNECTING
10 min.

Begin your group time with prayer. Ask God for willing hearts to receive his Word through this Bible study and for the courage to change as he challenges you in the weeks to come.

Deeper relationships happen when we take time to keep in touch with one another. As you begin, pass around a copy of the *Small Group Roster*, a sheet of paper, or one of you pass your study guide, opened to the *Small Group Roster*. When the roster gets to you, write down your contact information, including the best time and method for contacting you. Then, someone volunteer to make copies or type up a list with everyone's information and e-mail it to the group this week.

1. Begin this first session by introducing yourselves. Include your name, what you do for a living, what you do for fun, and anything else you would like to share.

2. Whether your group is new or ongoing, it's always important to reflect on and review your group values. In the *Appendix* is a *Small Group Agreement* with values most useful in sustaining healthy, balanced groups. Review these values and choose one or two—values you haven't previously focused on or have

room to grow in—to emphasize during this study. Choose those that will take your group to the next stage of intimacy and spiritual health. Discuss how you will implement these values in your small group.

3. In the Beatitudes, Jesus teaches what it means to be truly blessed. Describe a time when you felt truly blessed.

 GROWING   *45–50 min.*

Jesus begins his Sermon on the Mount by describing the attitudes and actions of kingdom-minded citizens. Then Jesus reminds his followers that they must be present in the world like salt and light, transforming others with the presence of God living in and through them.

Read Matthew 5:1–16.

4. Each of the Beatitudes begins with the word "blessed." Who is blessed according to these verses?

5. Discuss the point that Jesus makes in each of the Beatitudes and fill in the chart below.

Blessed are . . .	How does this apply to our lives?	How do we fall short?
The poor in spirit (v. 3)		
Those who mourn (v. 4)		
The meek (v. 5)		
Those who hunger and thirst for righteousness (v. 6)		

continued

Blessed are . . .	How does this apply to our lives?	How do we fall short?
The merciful (v. 7)		
The pure in heart (v. 8)		
The peacemakers (v. 9)		
Those persecuted because of righteousness (vv. 10–11)		

6. Why is it so difficult for a follower of Christ to put Jesus's words into practice?

What should we do to begin living as Jesus wants us to?

7. The following table shows the Beatitudes with the corresponding blessing that God gives those who live accordingly. How do each of these blessings relate to one another?

Blessed are...	The blessing
The poor in spirit (v. 3)	Theirs is the kingdom of heaven.
Those who mourn (v. 4)	They will be comforted.
The meek (v. 5)	They will inherit the earth.
Those who hunger and thirst for righteousness (v. 6)	They will be filled.
The merciful (v. 7)	They will be shown mercy.
The pure in heart (v. 8)	They will see God.
The peacemakers (v. 9)	They will be called children of God.
Those persecuted because of righteousness (vv. 10–11)	Theirs is the kingdom of heaven.

How will understanding these blessings help us live as kingdom-minded citizens?

18

8. Matthew 5:6 says: "Blessed are those who hunger and thirst for righteousness." *Righteousness* means "right standing with God." Based on the words of Jesus in the Beatitudes, what do you think hungering and thirsting for righteousness should look like in a Christian's life?

9. What substitutions do Christians tend to hunger for instead of righteousness?

   How can we overcome our hunger for these substitutes? (See 1 John 5:3–4 for insight.)

10. What do you think Jesus means by peacemakers in verse 9?

11. We are aliens in this world and will suffer persecution for standing up for God's standards of righteousness. What forms does this persecution take in our day-to-day lives?

    What can help you persevere when this happens?

12. What have you learned about your own attitudes during this session?

    What has God revealed to you?

13. Jesus tells us that living the Beatitudes will enable us to be *salt* and *light* (vv. 13–16), the transforming presence of God in the world today. What do you think it means to be salt and light? (See the *Study Notes* for information about salt and light.)

    How can living out these attitudes and actions help us to become salt and light?

The Beatitudes turn the world's values upside down and offer a vivid picture of true life in Christ. Fulfillment comes not through control, social status, possessions, or pleasure, but from purity of heart, a righteousness that can only be attained through faith in Jesus Christ, love, integrity, and hope in our consummation in God's kingdom. As we live out our transformation, we are provided un-limited access to God's bountiful grace that enables us to bring transformation to the lives of others—becoming kingdom-minded people who change the world.

DEVELOPING
10 min.

Kingdom-minded people who change the world do so through special gifts God has given us to use as the Holy Spirit leads. The first step in developing the gifts that God has given each of us is to deepen our relationship with him through prayer, reflection, and medita-tion on his Word.

14. Developing our ability to serve God as the Holy Spirit leads requires that we make time to let God speak to us daily. Which of the following next steps toward this goal are you willing to take for the next few weeks?

   ☐ *Prayer.* Commit to connecting with God daily through per-sonal prayer. It's important to separate yourself from the distractions in your life so you can really focus on commu-nicating with God. Some people find it helpful to write out their prayers in a journal.

   ☐ *Reflection.* At the end of each session you'll find *Reflections* Scriptures that specifically relate to the topic of our study for the session. These are provided to give you an opportunity for reading a short Bible passage five days a week during the course of this study. Write down your insights on what you read each day in the space provided. On the sixth day, summarize what God has shown you throughout the week.

   ☐ *Meditation.* Psalm 119:11 says: "I have hidden your word in my heart that I might not sin against you." Meditation is focused attention on the Word of God and is a great way to internalize God's Word more deeply. One way to do this is to write a portion of Scripture on a card and tape it somewhere where you're sure to see it often, such as your bathroom mirror, car's dashboard, or the kitchen table. Think about it as you get dressed in the morning, when you sit at red lights, or while you're eating a meal. Reflect on what God is saying to you through his words. Consider using the passages provided in the *Reflections* pages in each session. As you meditate upon these Scriptures, you will notice them beginning to take up residence in your heart and mind.

SHARING
10 min.

Jesus lived and died so that humankind might come to know him and be reconciled to God through him. Through his Holy Spirit, we are empowered to be his witnesses to the people around us.

15. Jesus wants all of his disciples to help others connect with him, to know him personally. When we live out the Beatitudes, we become like salt and light in the world (Matt. 5:13–16), transforming it with God's presence. How can focusing on the blessings Jesus talks about in the Beatitudes encourage us as we strive to be salt and light in the world?

16. In the weeks to come, you'll be asked to identify and share with people in your circle of influence who need to know Jesus or need to connect with him through a small group community. With this in mind, as you go about your day-to-day activities this week, pay special attention to the people God has placed in your life. There may be co-workers, family or friends, other parents at school or sporting events that you see or talk to on a regular basis. When we meet next time, we'll talk about how to help connect believers to Christian community and begin sharing Jesus with those who don't yet know him.

SURRENDERING
10 min.

Jeremiah 29:13 says, "You will seek me and find me when you seek me with all your heart." God promises to be there for us when we yield our hearts fully to him. Each week you will have a chance to surrender your hearts to God in worship and prayer.

17. Consider some different ways to worship that might fit your group. Following are a few ideas. Spend a few minutes worshiping God together.

☐ Have someone use their musical gifts to lead the group in a worship song. You might sing a simple chorus a cappella, with guitar/piano accompaniment, or with a worship CD.

☐ Read a passage of Scripture aloud together, making it a time of praise and worship as the words remind you of all God has done for you. Choose a psalm or other favorite verses.

☐ Spend a few minutes praising God aloud. You may highlight some of the attributes of God's character or praise him for specific circumstances in your life.

18. Every believer should have a plan for spending time alone with God. Your time with God is personal and reflects who you are in relationship with him. However you choose to spend your time with him, try to allow time for praise, prayer, and reading of Scripture. *Reflections* are provided at the end of each session for you to use as part of your daily time with God. These will offer reinforcement of the principles you are learning, and develop or strengthen your habit of time alone with God throughout the week.

19. Before you close your group in prayer, answer this question: "How can we pray for you this week?" Write prayer requests on your *Prayer and Praise Report* and commit to praying for each other throughout the week. Close in prayer asking God to encourage each participant to embrace the Beatitudes and begin to live them out daily.

Study Notes

Kingdom of heaven: God's people and the realm in which God reigns as King and his will is done. In the Sermon on the Mount, the King explains how citizens of his kingdom will live. "Kingdom of heaven" is a Jewish equivalent of "kingdom of God." Jews avoided saying God's name, so "heaven" became a way of referring to God. Matthew usually uses "kingdom of heaven," while Mark and Luke speak of the "kingdom of God."

Salt: Salt is used as a preservative and flavor enhancer. As a preservative, it hinders the spread of evil. As a flavor enhancer, it makes living in this world more palatable. The salt of the Dead Sea region was full of impurities and would often lose its flavor and effectiveness as a preservative.

Light: Light shines in stark contrast to the darkness. Followers of Christ are to be light, to stand out as positive witnesses, clearly visible in the dark world.

For Deeper Study (Optional)

In Luke 6:20–26, we find teaching by Jesus that parallels Matthew's Beatitudes and includes a point-by-point counterpart to each blessing. Read Luke 6:24–26. "But woe to you who are rich, for you have already received your comfort. Woe to you who are well fed now, for you will go hungry. Woe to you who laugh now, for you will mourn and weep. Woe to you when all men speak well of you, for that is how their fathers treated the false prophets."

1. Why do you think woes come upon those who are rich, well-fed, happy, and popular in life?

2. How does this further illustrate the truth that Christ's followers are blessed if we are kingdom-minded?

Reflections

Reading, reflecting, and meditating on the Word of God is essential to getting to know him deeply. As you read the verses each day, give prayerful consideration to what you learn about God, his Spirit, and his place in your life. Then record your thoughts, insights, or prayer in the *Reflect* section below the verses you read. On the sixth day, record a summary of what you learned over the entire week through this study.

Day 1. Finally, all of you, live in harmony with one another; be sympathetic, love as brothers, be compassionate and humble (1 Peter 3:8).

REFLECT

_____

_____

_____

_____

Day 2. Flee the evil desires of youth, and pursue righteousness, faith, love and peace, along with those who call on the Lord out of a pure heart (2 Tim. 2:22).

REFLECT

_____

_____

_____

_____

Day 3. Do nothing out of selfish ambition or vain conceit, but in humility consider others better than yourselves. Each of you should look not only to your own interests, but also to the interests of others (Phil. 2:3–4).

REFLECT

_____

_____

_____

_____

Day 4. But seek first his kingdom and his righteousness, and all these things will be given to you as well (Matt. 6:33).

REFLECT

_____

_____

_____

_____

Day 5. You are the salt of the earth. But if the salt loses its saltiness, how can it be made salty again? It is no longer good for anything, except to be thrown out and trampled by men (Matt. 5:13).

REFLECT

_____

_____

_____

_____

Day 6. Use the following space to write any insight God has put in your heart and mind about the things we have looked at in this session and during your _Reflections_ time this week.

SUMMARY

_____

_____

_____

_____

HOW GOOD IS GOOD ENOUGH?

MEMORY VERSE: Be perfect, therefore, as your heavenly Father is perfect (Matt. 5:48).

The town of Dedham is a small Massachusetts community. Their library holds over twenty thousand volumes on the history of Dedham with genealogy and local history. The Historical Society has an extensive manuscript holding with Dedham church and civic records dating back to the year 1635, newspapers from 1796, and an outstanding eighteenth-to-twentieth-century map collection. But amidst this massive treasury of books and records, the town aspired to be known in a greater sense—they wanted to be listed in the *Guinness World Records* book.

So on September 28, 2003, the town of Dedham held their annual Dedham Day in the town's memorial park. In addition to the usual food, fun, and cow chip bingo, the town held a limbo dance competition. With over 700 participants the town aspired to enter the Guinness book with the largest number of people participating in a limbo dance.

A fifteen-year-old resident, Kayala Costa, won the contest showing "how low she could go" by dancing under a 23-inch-high pole.

At that time, Kayala was slated to win a prize and a certificate for winning "the world's largest limbo dance contest."

Unfortunately, although the town of Dedham had achieved a feat unparalleled and their efforts should have earned the prestigious prize, their petition to the Guinness book was denied. They had failed to meet the most demanding standards. Guinness World Records had strict rules and regulations of competition that had to be met in order for a competitor to even qualify to attempt a world record.

The Mosaic Law was even more stringent. It set the bar and established God's righteous standards. It also established how impossible it is for us to attain salvation through our own abilities and self-righteousness. Like the prize, we could never earn our salvation through our efforts.

In this session we will discuss how Jesus did not come to abolish the law but to fulfill it—how he lived out God's standard for perfection—and how we, through his life and death, believing in faith, can attain the prize of everlasting life and salvation through him.

CONNECTING   *10 min.*

Open your group with prayer. Invite the Holy Spirit to remove any uncertainty that you may have in the power of God to transform your heart.

1. If you have new people joining you for the first time, take a few minutes to briefly introduce yourselves.

2. What do you think it means to be "perfect"? Discuss whether or not you think it is possible to attain what you've described.

GROWING   *45–50 min.*

The Mosaic Law set the bar high for our behavior. It not only shows us who God is and how he wants us to live, but it demonstrates, through its perfection, our inability to live by God's righteous standards on our own, and therefore leads us to depend on him for salvation. Jesus did not come to abolish the perfect law but to fulfill it in his life and death. As Jesus connects the original intention of the law to the dawning kingdom of heaven, he upholds its deep, underlying meanings.

Read Matthew 5:17–48.

3. What do we learn about the Law in verses 17–19?

4. What do you think Jesus means when he says, "Unless your righteousness surpasses that of the Pharisees and the teachers of the law, you will certainly not enter the kingdom of heaven" (v. 20). (See the *Study Notes* for information about the "Pharisees.")

5. Where does this righteousness come from (see Rom. 3:22–24)?

   How does it feel to know this is possible for you?

6. What is Jesus teaching about the relationship between anger and murder (Matt. 5:21–22)?

   Why do you think Jesus makes this strong connection?

7. Jesus commands us to reconcile our anger quickly. Why do you think quick reconciliation is so important?

8. At what point does adultery occur, according to Matthew 5:28?

   How can you protect yourself from this?

9. Jesus is using hyperbole to illustrate the effects of sin (vv. 29–30). Under the law, sin results in death, and therefore should be dealt with very drastically—not taking it lightly. Give an example of how one might deal drastically with a sin in their life.

10. Why does Jesus teach against swearing oaths in verses 33–37?

    How can we benefit from speaking simply and truthfully?

11. The law regarding retaliation (v. 38) was established to ensure that punishment was just and in proportion to the crime. Jesus calls us to return the evil that others do to us with good. What do you think about this?

    What must we do if we are to embrace this teaching to not resist the evil person?

12. In verses 43–48, Jesus calls us to love even our enemies, since God loved us when we were his enemies. Who are the enemies of the church today? Why is it difficult to love them?

    Verse 44 tells us to pray for those who persecute us. Why is prayer important in dealing with our enemies?

13. In each of the six examples that Jesus gives us in Matthew 5:21–48, he quotes from the Old Testament Law, or a traditional interpretation of the law, and then interprets it based on the heart of God. What do you learn about actions and motives from this passage?

14. Jesus says in verse 48: "Be perfect, therefore, as your heavenly Father is perfect." *Perfect* implies being fully developed morally. How can we be obedient to this command to be perfect?

    According to verses 43–47, what must we do to attain perfection?

    In what ways can loving as Christ describes change our lives?

While the law set the bar high for our behavior, God did not leave us without hope to reach it. Jesus lived out God's standard for perfection and satisfied the requirements of the law. Through his perfect life and sacrifice on the cross, and the power of the Holy Spirit to live surrendered to him, we can be good enough.

DEVELOPING   *10 min.*

Accountability means being answerable to another for our actions. Spiritual accountability happens when we invite someone into our life for the purpose of encouraging our faith journey and challenging us in specific areas of desired growth. Hebrews 3:12–13 says: "See to it, brothers, that none of you has a sinful, unbelieving heart that turns away from the living God. But encourage one another daily, as long as it is called Today, so that none of you may be hardened by sin's deceitfulness." Opening our lives to someone and making ourselves vulnerable to their loving admonition could perhaps be one of the most difficult things to do; however, it could also result in the deepest and most lasting spiritual growth we've known.

15. Scripture tells us in Ephesians 4:25: "Laying aside falsehood, speak truth, each one of you with his neighbor, for we are members of one another" (NASB). With this in mind, take a moment to pair up with someone in your group to be your spiritual partner for the remainder of this study. We strongly recommend men partner with men, and women with women. (Refer to the *Leader's Notes* for this question in the *Appendix* for information on what it means to be a spiritual partner.)

    Turn to the *Personal Health Plan* in the *Appendix*. In the box that says, "WHO are you connecting with spiritually?" write your partner's name.

    In the box that says, "WHAT is your next step for growth?" write one step you would like to take for growth during this study. Tell your partner what step you chose. When you check in with your partner each meeting, the "Partner's Progress" column on this chart will provide a place to record your partner's progress in the goal he or she chose.

16. Spending time together outside of group meetings helps to build stronger relationships within your group as you get to know each other better. Discuss whether your group would like to have a potluck or other type of social to celebrate together what God is doing in your group. You could plan to share a meal prior to a group meeting or plan to follow your comple-

tion of this study with a meal together—maybe a barbecue. Appoint one or two people who can follow up with everyone outside of group time to put a plan together.

SHARING   *10 min.*

The people in your life with whom you come into regular contact make up your circles of influence or *Circles of Life*.

17. Take a look at the *Circles of Life* diagram below and think of people you know in each category who need to be connected in Christian community. Write the names of two or three people in each circle.

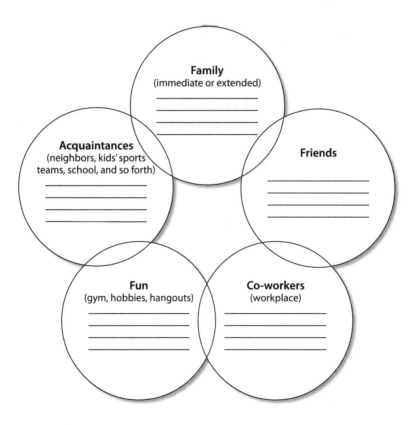

The people who fill these circles are not there by accident. God has strategically placed each of them within your sphere of influence because he has equipped you to minister to them and share with them in ways no one else can. Consider the following ideas for reaching out to one or two of the people you listed and make a plan to follow through with them this week.

☐ This is a wonderful time to welcome a few friends into your group. Which of the people you listed could you invite? It's possible that you may need to help your friend overcome obstacles to coming to a place where he or she can encounter Jesus. Does your friend need a ride to the group or help with child care?

☐ Consider inviting a friend to attend a weekend church service with you and possibly plan to enjoy a meal together afterward. This can be a great opportunity to talk with someone about your faith in Jesus.

☐ Is there someone who is unable to attend your group or church but who still needs a connection? Would you be willing to have lunch or coffee with that person, catch up on life, and share something you've learned from this study? Jesus doesn't call all of us to lead small groups, but he does call every disciple to spiritually multiply his or her life over time.

 ## SURRENDERING *10 min.*

Deuteronomy 32:3–4 declares: "I will proclaim the name of the LORD. Oh, praise the greatness of our God! He is the Rock, his works are perfect, and all his ways are just." Only our perfect God is worthy of praise.

18. Focus on the words of David as you read Psalm 145 aloud together in an attitude of corporate worship.

19. Take a few minutes to talk about what it would take to make time with God a priority every day or even five or six days a week. Don't put time demands on yourself at first; just make

it a priority to draw near to God for a few minutes each day and gradually you will desire more. Use the *Reflections* at the end of each session as a starting point.

20. Share your prayer requests as a group. Be sure to record everyone's requests on your *Prayer and Praise Report*. Use these as reminders to pray for everyone throughout the week.

    After sharing, gather in smaller circles of three or four people to pray for one another. Be careful not to pressure anyone who may not be comfortable praying aloud. When you pray for each person, you may find it meaningful to hold hands or place your hands on each other's shoulders. Jesus often touched people to communicate his care for them.

Study Notes

Abolish . . . fulfill: Jesus fulfilled the Law of Moses by living out God's perfect standard of righteousness, by explaining its meaning for kingdom citizens, and by dying on the cross to satisfy the penalty for sin required by the law. His death replaced the animal sacrifices that the Law commanded. This does not mean there is no longer a need for the biblical books of Moses; they are still God's Word, and they apply to us in the way Jesus interprets them.

Pharisees: The Pharisees were a lay movement of Judaism that took the traditions of the elders and Old Testament purity laws for hereditary priests and developed a system for laypeople to practice them. They wore distinguishable clothing so as to be easily recognized. They were experts in interpreting Scripture. Though they were not official clergy, their study and practice of the Law made them religious authorities. They were the most influential of the sects of Judaism and highly regarded. They strictly adhered to OT law and traditions of elders, with particular focus on righteous behavior. They bitterly opposed Jesus and his teachings. Their limited understanding of God and Scripture blinded them to true life in Christ.

The Pharisees' primary goal was for the whole nation to be as pure and holy as the priesthood. Their system included the application of biblical laws to everyday life. They focused on outward behaviors that a dedicated person could reasonably live up to (and they could offer sacrifices for sin when they failed). But following their system required great dedication, and the idea of being more righteous than a Pharisee would have seemed superhuman to Jesus's audience. And in truth, Jesus's idea of righteousness—which involves not just outward behaviors but clean motives, desires, and thoughts—is superhuman. It requires supernatural help.

You have heard. . . : Jesus takes a series of commands from the Law of Moses and explains how he interprets and applies them. His interpretations consistently go deeper than the interpretations of the Pharisees and other teachers of the law.

Divorce: Moses's teaching in Deuteronomy 24:1–4 offered a concession for a "certificate of divorce" in response to people's hardness of heart (Mark 10:5). This was instituted to protect the interests of the affected woman and family, not to legalize, condone, or justify divorce. Some rabbis errantly concluded that it was acceptable for men to divorce their wives so long as they gave them the required certificate of divorce.

For Deeper Study (Optional)

Read Romans 13:9–10: "The commandments, 'Do not commit adultery,' 'Do not murder,' 'Do not steal,' 'Do not covet,' and whatever other commandment there may be, are summed up in this one rule: 'Love your neighbor as yourself.' Love does no harm to its neighbor. Therefore love is the fulfillment of the law."

1. How can loving your neighbor as yourself serve as the fulfillment of the entire law?

Reflections

Hopefully last week you made a commitment to read, reflect, and meditate on the Word of God each day. Following are selections of Scripture provided as a starting point to drawing near to God through time with him. Read the daily verses and then record your thoughts, insights, or prayers in the space provided. On the sixth day, record a summary of what you have learned over the entire week through this study or use this space to write down how God has challenged you personally.

Day 1. I tell you the truth, until heaven and earth disappear, not the smallest letter, not the least stroke of a pen, will by any means disappear from the Law until everything is accomplished (Matt. 5:18).

REFLECT

_____

_____

_____

_____

Day 2. If your right eye causes you to sin, gouge it out and throw it away. It is better for you to lose one part of your body than for your whole body to be thrown into hell. And if your right hand causes you to sin, cut it off and throw it away. It is better for you to lose one part of your body than for your whole body to go into hell (Matt. 5:29–30).

REFLECT

_____

_____

_____

_____

Day 3. Simply let your "Yes" be "Yes," and your "No," "No"; anything beyond this comes from the evil one (Matt. 5:37).

REFLECT

_____

_____

_____

_____

Day 4. But I tell you: Love your enemies and pray for those who persecute you, that you may be sons of your Father in heaven. He causes his sun to rise on the evil and the good, and sends rain on the righteous and the unrighteous (Matt. 5:44–45).

REFLECT

_____

_____

_____

_____

Day 5. For I tell you that unless your righteousness surpasses that of the Pharisees and the teachers of the law, you will certainly not enter the kingdom of heaven (Matt. 5:20).

REFLECT

_____

_____

_____

_____

Day 6. Use this space to record insights, thoughts, or prayers that God has given you during *Session Two* and your *Reflections* time.

SUMMARY

_____

_____

_____

_____

AN AUDIENCE OF ONE

MEMORY VERSE: Be careful not to do your "acts of righteousness" before men, to be seen by them. If you do, you will have no reward from your Father in heaven (Matt. 6:1).

When Joshua was four years old, he was terribly self-conscious. When other kids were acting silly, doing somersaults, or making funny faces, he would stand by and watch with rapt attention. But if asked to join in the game, he would say, "No!" and run off to his bedroom. But if you peeked around the corner, you'd find him making faces at his own reflection in the mirror or somersaulting over and over again where no one else could see him. Joshua wouldn't even consider trying something new in front of other people until he knew for certain that he could do it well. He wanted to impress them, not be laughed at for failing.

Even though Joshua thought so, the other kids didn't care how well he could play along. They just wanted him to loosen up and be part of the fun.

We won't likely be asked to do somersaults or make silly faces, but we may be asked to do things for God's kingdom such as close the group in prayer, invite a friend to church, serve in a ministry, or give to the needy. We may be tempted to let what others will think of us prevent us from getting involved, but what God wants is for us to serve him—only him. God doesn't care how well we do the things we do for him; he delights in seeing us strip off our inhibitions and be vulnerable before him, performing to our individual best, not to impress others with our gifts and abilities, but for his pleasure and for the sake of furthering his kingdom.

In this session, we will discuss Jesus's teachings about the motives that underlie our behavior. We should never allow what others think of us to become our reasons for obeying God. Our acts of righteousness should be outward demonstrations of our inner heart toward God.

CONNECTING

10 min.

Begin your group discussion time by praying Psalm 86:11, which says: "Teach me your way, O LORD, and I will walk in your truth; give me an undivided heart, that I may fear your name."

1. Most people want to live a healthy, balanced life. A regular medical checkup is a good way to measure health and spot potential problems. In the same way, a spiritual checkup is vital to your spiritual well-being. The *Personal Health Assessment* was designed to give you a quick snapshot, or pulse, of your spiritual health.

   Take a few minutes alone to complete the *Personal Health Assessment*, found in the *Appendix*. After answering each question, tally your results. Then, pair up with your spiritual partner and briefly share one purpose that is going well and one that needs a little work. Then go to the *Personal Health Plan* and record one next step you plan to take in the area of the purpose you want to work on. If you haven't established your spiritual partnership yet, do it now. (Refer to the *Session Two Leader's Notes* in the *Developing* section for help.)

2. Have you ever done something in secret, like planned a surprise party, worked behind the scenes on a project, or given an

anonymous donation? If so, share about how that experience made you feel.

GROWING

Giving to the needy, praying, and fasting have been called the "three pillars" of Jewish acts of righteousness. In Matthew 6:1–18, Jesus is not addressing the actions themselves, but the underlying motives for them.

Read Matthew 6:1–18.

3. In this portion of Scripture, Jesus focuses on our "acts of righteousness." What do we learn about how and why we should give, pray, and fast?

   What does this teach us about who should be honored by our giving, prayer, and fasting?

4. Jesus says: "Be careful not to do your 'acts of righteousness' before men, to be seen by them. If you do, you will have no reward from your Father in heaven" (v. 1). Why are our "acts of righteousness" before others not rewarded in heaven?

5. What do you think Jesus means when he says "do not let your left hand know what your right hand is doing" (v. 3)? How can we obey the spirit of this command?

6. In verse 6, Jesus teaches that we should go behind closed doors to pray to our Father who is unseen. Why do you believe it's important to pray in secret?

7. Jesus is not necessarily condemning long prayers in verse 7. What do you think he is warning against?

   How can we guard against this in our own prayer life?

8. If our Father knows what we need before we ask him (v. 8), then why is it necessary to pray?

9. Unlike the rambling prayers of the pagans, the Lord's Prayer is pointed and concise. Look at the petitions given in Jesus's model prayer in verses 9–13 in the chart below.

The orientation	The petition	The application
	Our Father (v. 9)	Who are we talking to? The One who is always near and who cares for our needs.
	Hallowed be your name (v. 9)	Prayer should begin in worship of God and his holy name.
Oriented to God	Your kingdom come (v. 10)	We should pray for the advancement of God's kingdom until the time of its consummation.
	Your will be done (v. 10)	We should pray according to his will, for the things we know he wants done.
	Give us today our daily bread (v. 11)	We should pray for the daily provision for our physical needs.
	Forgive us our debts (v. 12)	We should pray for the daily provision for our spiritual needs—grace, forgiveness, etc.
Oriented to Self	As we also have forgiven our debtors (v. 12)	We should extend the same grace and mercy toward others that we have received from God.
	Lead us not into temptation (v. 13)	We should pray that we may be protected from and strengthened during our temptation to sin.

What does this type of thoughtful prayer demonstrate about the attitudes of the person who prays it?

10. Jesus is saying forgiveness is evidence of his saving grace in us when he says: "If you forgive men when they sin against you, your heavenly Father will also forgive you. But if you do not forgive men their sins, your Father will not forgive your sins" (vv. 14–15).

    How might our inability to offer forgiveness to others affect our testimony to God's forgiveness for our own sins?

11. Why do you think Jesus is concerned with our appearance while fasting (vv. 16–18)?

12. The Bible teaches us to fast. Should fasting be a part of worship today? Why do you think so?

13. Jesus's teachings show us he is focused on the heart motives behind our actions. How can we ensure that we are giving, praying, and fasting with pure motives?

The "acts of righteousness" by which we demonstrate outwardly our love for God should be motivated by deep thankfulness for what God has done and continues to do in our lives. We must be careful to never allow the things we do in obedience to God to become about appearing virtuous and impressive to others. We must remember "the LORD does not look at the things man looks at. Man looks at the outward appearance, but the LORD looks at the heart" (1 Sam. 16:7).

DEVELOPING

10 min.

Giving our hearts to God extends to loving his people. Galatians 5:13 says: "Serve one another in love." This is not optional. Our automobiles need all of their parts to run smoothly, and so does the body of Christ. God designed each of us uniquely to fill specific needs within the church. The infinite needs of countless people and circumstances around us require that we use our unique gifts in service to God and others.

14. Discuss some of the ways that we can serve the body of Christ. Is there a particular area of service that God has put on your heart to serve either this group or in your local church? If not, investigate the opportunities and pray about finding a ministry in which you can serve. As you take that first step, God will lead you to the ministry that expresses your passion.

15. On your *Personal Health Plan,* next to the "Develop" icon, answer the "WHERE are you serving?" question. If you are

not currently serving, note one area where you will consider serving.

SHARING   10 *min.*

Everyone searches for significance and purpose in life. The prophet Jeremiah offers encouragement in Jeremiah 29:11. It says: "'For I know the plans I have for you,' declares the LORD, 'plans to prosper you and not to harm you, plans to give you hope and a future.'" We can claim this promise as God's children. Sadly, many miss the opportunity to know God and the hope he gives. As we share God's love with others, we can offer true significance and purpose to them by introducing them to the One who promises to give it.

16. In the last session you were asked to write some names in the *Circles of Life* diagram. Go back to the *Circles of Life* diagram to remind yourself of the various people you come into contact with on a regular basis. Have you followed up with those you identified who need to connect with other Christians? If not, when will you contact them?

17. If you have never invited Jesus to take control of your life, why not ask him now? If you are not clear about God's gift of eternal life for everyone who believes in Jesus and how to receive this gift, take a minute to pray and ask God to help you understand what he wants you to do about trusting in Jesus.

SURRENDERING   10 *min.*

James 5:16 says: "Confess your sins to each other and pray for each other so that you may be healed. The prayer of a righteous man is powerful and effective."

18. Take some time now to begin the *Circle of Prayer* exercise. This exercise allows for focused prayer over each person or couple in the group. Each person or couple will have an opportunity to share any pressing needs, concerns, or struggles

requiring prayer, and the rest of the group will pray for these requests. More complete instructions for this can be found in the *Leader's Notes*.

For Deeper Study (Optional)

Read Isaiah 58:3–9. "Yet on the day of your fasting, you do as you please and exploit all your workers. Your fasting ends in quarreling and strife, and in striking each other with wicked fists. You cannot fast as you do today and expect your voice to be heard on high. Is this the kind of fast I have chosen, only a day for a man to humble himself? Is it only for bowing one's head like a reed and for lying on sackcloth and ashes? Is that what you call a fast, a day acceptable to the LORD?

"Is not this the kind of fasting I have chosen: to loose the chains of injustice and untie the cords of the yoke, to set the oppressed free and break every yoke? Is it not to share your food with the hungry and to provide the poor wanderer with shelter—when you see the naked, to clothe him, and not to turn away from your own flesh and blood? Then your light will break forth like the dawn, and your healing will quickly appear; then your righteousness will go before you, and the glory of the LORD will be your rear guard. Then you will call, and the LORD will answer; you will cry for help, and he will say: Here am I."

1. For what are the people reprimanded?

2. How does the prophet describe the outward evidence of true righteousness?

3. What more do we learn from this passage about God's heart toward our "acts of righteousness"?

Reflections

If you've been spending time each day connecting with God through his Word, congratulations! Some experts say that it takes 21 repetitions to develop a new habit. By the end of this week, you'll be well on your way to cultivating new spiritual habits that will encourage you in your walk with God. This week, continue to read the daily verses, giving prayerful consideration to what you learn about God, his Spirit, and his place in your life. Then, as before, record your thoughts, insights, or prayers in the space provided. On the sixth day, record a summary of what you have learned throughout the week.

Day 1. Be careful not to do your "acts of righteousness" before men, to be seen by them. If you do, you will have no reward from your Father in heaven (Matt. 6:1).

REFLECT

_____

_____

_____

_____

Day 2. But when you give to the needy, do not let your left hand know what your right hand is doing, so that your giving may be in secret. Then your Father, who sees what is done in secret, will reward you (Matt. 6:3–4).

REFLECT

_____

_____

_____

_____

Day 3. This, then, is how you should pray: "Our Father in heaven, hallowed be your name, your kingdom come, your will be done on earth as it is in heaven. Give us today our daily bread. Forgive us our debts, as we also have forgiven our debtors. And lead us not into temptation, but deliver us from the evil one" (Matt. 6:9–13).

REFLECT

_____

_____

_____

_____

Day 4. Do not be quick with your mouth, do not be hasty in your heart to utter anything before God. God is in heaven and you are on earth, so let your words be few (Eccles. 5:2).

REFLECT

_____

_____

_____

_____

Day 5. You were taught, with regard to your former way of life, to put off your old self, which is being corrupted by its deceitful desires; to be made new in the attitude of your minds; and to put on the new self, created to be like God in true righteousness and holiness (Eph. 4:22–24).

REFLECT

_____

_____

_____

_____

Day 6. Record your weekly summary of what God has shown you in the space below.

SUMMARY

_____

_____

_____

_____

HOW TO THRIVE IN ANY ECONOMY

MEMORY VERSE: But seek first his kingdom and his righteousness, and all these things will be given to you as well (Matt. 6:33).

While returning home from a camping trip over the Fourth of July weekend, the family looked out the car window and down the familiar street to see the charred remains of their neighbor's house. An accident involving fireworks had totally devastated the home. Not a fiber of carpet, a stitch of clothing, or a crumb from the pantry remained. Reports said the fire burned uncontrollably for only about fifteen minutes, but in that time had devoured everything from the roof to the crawlspace. The victim's furniture, clothing, housewares, and personal treasures were all gone.

While this catastrophic event destroyed every possession that family owned, it did not destroy their faith. In spite of the pain they felt as a result of their great and total loss, they did not despair. They held firm to their belief that no matter what happens on this earth, God is in control. Their confidence remains in the God who provided for their past, to bring ultimate restoration to their future—to turn their tragedy into triumph.

We may be tempted to believe that there can be no recovering from total destruction of all of our earthly belongings, but the truth of God's Word promises there is more to live for than material possessions: hope for an eternally secure home with the Father if we will become seekers of his kingdom first.

In this session, Jesus teaches us the proper perspective for the concerns of this life and how to become people who seek God's kingdom first.

CONNECTING

10 min.

Open your group with thanks to God for what he has taught you during the last few weeks of your study of the *Sermon on the Mount*. Pray also that God would open the eyes of your hearts to see his truth today.

1. Take five minutes to check in with your spiritual partner or with another partner if yours is absent. Share with your partner how your time with God went this week. What is one thing you discovered? Or, what obstacles hindered you from following through? Turn to your *Personal Health Plan*. Make a note about your partner's progress and how you can pray for him or her.

2. Have you ever received an unexpected financial or material blessing? If yes, share what happened.

GROWING

45–50 min.

From issues of personal integrity, Jesus turns to the matter of developing a heavenly mindset.

Read Matthew 6:19–34.

3. What is Jesus teaching us about the worries of this life through this passage?

4. Describe Jesus's attitude toward material possessions in verses 19–21.

5. Why do you think our attitudes about money and possessions are so important to our spiritual well-being?

   What then should our attitudes be?

6. Give some examples of how to store up "treasures in heaven" (v. 20).

7. In verse 21 Jesus said: "For where your treasure is, there your heart will be also." Give some examples of how this truth is evident in our lives.

   What can we do to ensure that our hearts remain properly focused?

8. Jesus says if our eyes are good, our whole body will be full of light, but if our eyes are bad our bodies will be full of darkness (vv. 22–23).

   What do you think this means?

   How can we keep our eyes "good"?

9. Verse 24 says: "You cannot serve both God and Money." Why isn't it possible to serve both God and money?

10. God has more than enough resources to meet our needs. What kinds of things do we tend to worry about which should be entrusted to God (vv. 25–32)?

    Why is it so difficult to trust God with these things?

11. Jesus accuses those who worry of having little faith (v. 30). How is our anxiety evidence of a lack of faith in God?

How can living a life influenced by Jesus's financial principles in verses 19–34 help you to live without worry?

12. The antidote to selfishness and worry is to seek God's kingdom first. What does seeking God's kingdom first look like in a typical person's life?

How is this effective at combating our selfish and worrisome ways?

13. What is the result of seeking God's kingdom first, according to verse 33?

What are "all these things" to which Jesus is referring?

As we learn to shift the focus of our time and resources from earthly concerns to heavenly concerns, we can be assured not only of God's provision for us here on earth but of our eternal security as well.

DEVELOPING   *10 min.*

First Peter 4:10 says: "Each one should use whatever gift he has received to serve others, faithfully administering God's grace in its various forms." Last session we talked about using our God-given gifts to serve him in the body of Christ. Today we will spend some time exploring the gifts we are given.

14. The Bible lists the many spiritual gifts given to believers. Take five minutes and review the *Spiritual Gifts Inventory* in the *Appendix*. Discuss which of the listed gifts you believe you may have. If you are unsure, you can review the inventory with a trusted friend who knows you well. Chances are they have witnessed one or more of these gifts in your life.

Once you have an idea about what your spiritual gifts may be, discuss how you may be able to use them in ministry. Plan to investigate the opportunities available to you in your church and get involved in serving the body of Christ. It's amazing to experience God using you to fill a specific need within his church.

15. Briefly discuss the future of your group. How many of you are willing to stay together as a group and work through another study? If you have time, turn to the *Small Group Agreement* and talk about any changes you would like to make as you move forward as a group.

SHARING   *10 min.*

One of the ways we can store up treasures in heaven is by sharing the good news with others and helping them to grow in their new relationship with Christ.

16. In *Session Two*, you identified people within your *Circles of Life* that needed connection to Christian community. Jesus's commission in Acts 1:8 included sharing him not only within our own circles of influence (our Jerusalem), but also in Judea and Samaria and the ends of the earth. Judea included the region in which Jerusalem was located. Today, this might include neighboring communities or cities. As a group, discuss the following possible actions you can take to share Jesus with your Judea in a tangible way.

   ☐ Collect new blankets and/or socks for the homeless. Bring them with you next week and have someone deliver them to a ministry serving the homeless.

   ☐ Bring nonperishable food items to the next group meeting and designate one person to donate them to a local food bank.

   ☐ As a group, pick a night to volunteer to serve meals at a mission or homeless shelter.

SURRENDERING   *10 min.*

First Peter 1:22 says: "Love one another deeply, from the heart." One way we love one another deeply is to pray focused prayer over each other's needs.

17. Last week you began praying for the specific needs of each person or couple in the group during the *Circle of Prayer* exercise. Take some time now to pray over those for whom the group hasn't yet prayed.

For Deeper Study (Optional)

Read 1 Timothy 6:9–10. "People who want to get rich fall into temptation and a trap and into many foolish and harmful desires that plunge men into ruin and destruction. For the love of money is a root of all kinds of evil. Some people, eager for money, have wandered from the faith and pierced themselves with many griefs."

1. How is the love for money a source of temptation?

2. In what ways does this love of money "plunge men into ruin and destruction"?

Now read 1 Timothy 6:17–19. "Command those who are rich in this present world not to be arrogant nor to put their hope in wealth, which is so uncertain, but to put their hope in God, who richly provides us with everything for our enjoyment. Command them to do good, to be rich in good deeds, and to be generous and willing to share. In this way they will lay up treasure for themselves as a firm foundation for the coming age, so that they may take hold of the life that is truly life."

1. Why should we not place hope in riches?

2. What should we do instead?

3. What does this passage teach us about what God values?

Reflections

Second Timothy 3:16–17 reads: "All Scripture is God-breathed and is useful for teaching, rebuking, correcting and training in righteousness, so that the man of God may be thoroughly equipped for every good work." Allow God's Word to train you in righteousness as you read, reflect on, and respond to the Scripture.

Day 1. Do not store up for yourselves treasures on earth, where moth and rust destroy, and where thieves break in and steal. But store up for yourselves treasures in heaven, where moth and rust do not destroy, and where thieves do not break in and steal (Matt. 6:19–20).

REFLECT

_____

_____

_____

_____

Day 2. For where your treasure is, there your heart will be also (Matt. 6:21).

REFLECT

_____

_____

_____

_____

Day 3. No one can serve two masters. Either he will hate the one and love the other, or he will be devoted to the one and despise the other. You cannot serve both God and Money (Matt. 6:24).

REFLECT

_____

_____

_____

_____

Day 4. Who of you by worrying can add a single hour to his life? (Matt. 6:27).

REFLECT

_____

_____

_____

_____

Day 5. Therefore do not worry about tomorrow, for tomorrow will worry about itself. Each day has enough trouble of its own (Matt. 6:34).

REFLECT

_____

_____

_____

_____

Day 6. Record your weekly summary of what God has shown you in the space below.

SUMMARY

_____

_____

_____

_____

A MORE PERFECT YOU

MEMORY VERSE: So in everything, do to others what you would have them do to you, for this sums up the Law and the Prophets (Matt. 7:12).

Mother Teresa of Calcutta said, "I have found the paradox, that if you love until it hurts, there can be no more hurt, only more love." Love is the foundation of our relationship with God. Scripture tells us: God is love (1 John 4:8); love comes from God (1 John 4:7); he so loved the world (John 3:16); and he first loved us (1 John 4:19). Peter says, "Love covers over a multitude of sins" (1 Peter 4:8).

There is no denying it: loving relationships work! Loving until it hurts doesn't leave room for selfish motives or judgmental hearts. It offers forbearance, forgiveness, and grace. By depending on God and the power of the Holy Spirit to love until it hurts, we can begin to live righteously toward God and others.

In this session, Jesus teaches us how to live in relationship with God and one another.

CONNECTING

10 min.

Psalm 100:4 says: "Enter his gates with thanksgiving and his courts with praise; give thanks to him and praise his name." As you begin your time together, offer a prayer of thanksgiving for all that God has done so far in your small group. Ask him to open your heart to receive his message for you today.

1. Check in with your spiritual partner or with another partner if yours is absent. Talk about any challenges you are currently facing in reaching the goals you have set throughout this study. Tell your spiritual partner how he or she has helped you follow through with each step. Be sure to write down your partner's progress.

2. Have you ever considered that something you do might be a blessing to someone simply because you would appreciate it yourself? Share something you did that was a blessing to someone else and how it made you feel.

GROWING

45–50 min.

Jesus continues his sermon on the mount by telling his disciples more about how to live in relationship with others and with God.

Read Matthew 7:1–12.

3. What does this passage teach us about how we should treat others?

4. Again, Jesus zeroes in on the motivation or attitude behind our actions. What attitudes does he warn against in verses 1–5?

5. Why do you think Jesus used the term "plank" or "log" (NASB) to describe our sin (v. 3), yet used "speck" to describe the sins of others?

6. What do you think Jesus means when he says, "Do not give dogs what is sacred" or "do not throw your pearls to pigs" (v. 6)? See the *Study Notes* for more about dogs and pigs.

   Why do you think Jesus issues this warning?

7. Jesus has given many heart issues to address, and now he encourages us to pray about these things. Matthew 7:7 says: "Keep on asking, and you will be given what you ask for. Keep on looking, and you will find. Keep on knocking, and the door will be opened" (NLT). Why is "keep on" important?

   What obstacles can hinder us from praying in this way?

8. What reason does verse 11 give for asking God to meet our needs?

9. Why do you think God wants us to ask him for what he already knows we need?

10. Based on Jesus's example of the parent's provision of bread and fish, what are the "good gifts" Jesus promises?

11. Verse 12 has become known as "the Golden Rule." It sums up the Law and the Prophets (the whole Old Testament) and therefore simplifies into one statement how to live righteously. How is it possible to live out this "rule" in our day-to-day lives, not only in action but in attitude?

We are to treat others with the same generous but discerning spirit that we would like them to use with us, and we are to pray persistently with confidence in God's good heart. By depending on the power of the Holy Spirit to do these things, we can live righteously toward God and others.

DEVELOPING

10 min.

During the previous four weeks, hopefully you've developed some new growth disciplines such as accountability, Scripture memorization, meditation on the Word of God, and daily time with God. Consider taking your commitment to know God better one step further this week.

12. If you've been spending time each day in personal focused prayer, doing *Reflections*, and/or meditating on God's Word, consider taking your commitment a step further this week by journaling. Read through *Journaling 101* found in the *Appendix*. Commit this week to spending a portion of your time with God journaling.

13. During *Session Two*, you should have discussed whether your group would like to have a potluck or social. Take a few minutes now to tie up any loose ends in your plan.

SHARING

10 min.

Jesus wanted his disciples to share his gospel not only with their local communities, but also the world. *You* can be involved in taking the gospel to *all* nations.

14. Next to the "Share" icon on your *Personal Health Plan*, answer the "WHEN are you shepherding another person in Christ?" question.

15. In previous sessions you were asked to identify people who need to be connected in Christian community. Return to the *Circles of Life* diagram. Outside each circle, write down one or two names of people you know who need to know Christ. Commit to praying for an opportunity to share Jesus with each of them. You may invite them to attend an outreach event with you, or you may feel led to share the good news with him or her over coffee. Share your commitment with your spiritual

partner. Pray together for God's Holy Spirit to give you the words to speak with boldness.

SURRENDERING

10 min.

Philippians 4:6 tells us: "Do not be anxious about anything, but in everything, by prayer and petition, with thanksgiving, present your requests to God." Prayer represents a powerful act of surrender to the Lord as we put aside our pride and lay our burdens at his feet.

16. During the past two weeks, you've been praying for the specific needs of each person or couple in the group during the *Circle of Prayer* exercise. Take some time now to pray over those for whom the group hasn't yet prayed. As you did last week, allow each individual to share the specific needs or challenges they are facing. Ask for God's transforming power to bring change to their lives.

17. Turn to the *Personal Health Plan* and individually consider the "HOW are you surrendering your heart?" question. Look to the *Sample Personal Health Plan* for help. Share some of your thoughts with the group.

18. Spend a moment silently praying as David did in Psalm 139:23–24: "Search me, O God, and know my heart; test me and know my anxious thoughts. See if there is any offensive way in me, and lead me in the way everlasting." Once you feel you've entered into an attitude of worship, sing a worship song or read Psalm 139 aloud together.

Study Notes

Dogs and pigs: In Jesus's day, dogs were not common house pets, but wild, aggressive, and considered unclean. Pigs were also unclean for Jews, who were forbidden to eat pork. Pigs were often considered wild and dangerous. Together they represent what is to be despised. The dogs are hostile to what is sacred and turn on the giver, and the pigs trample the pearls underfoot.

For Deeper Study (Optional)

Read 1 Corinthians 5:9–13. "I have written you in my letter not to associate with sexually immoral people—not at all meaning the people of this world who are immoral, or the greedy and swindlers, or idolaters. In that case you would have to leave this world. But now I am writing you that you must not associate with anyone who calls himself a brother but is sexually immoral or greedy, an idolater or a slanderer, a drunkard or a swindler. With such a man do not even eat. What business is it of mine to judge those outside the church? Are you not to judge those inside? God will judge those outside. 'Expel the wicked man from among you.'"

1. What does this passage teach us about judging others?

2. Why is it important to hold believers accountable for their actions?

3. What do you think Paul means when he says in Galatians 5:9, "A little yeast works through the whole batch of dough"?

4. How can Christian accountability encourage you in your own walk with the Lord?

Reflections

The Lord promised Joshua success and prosperity in Joshua 1:8 when he said: "Do not let this Book of the Law depart from your mouth; meditate on it day and night, so that you may be careful to do everything written in it. Then you will be prosperous and successful." We too can claim this promise for our lives as we commit to meditate on the Word of God each day. As in previous weeks, read and meditate on the daily verses and record any insights you gain in the space provided. Summarize what you have learned this week on Day 6.

Day 1. For in the same way you judge others, you will be judged, and with the measure you use, it will be measured to you (Matt. 7:2).

REFLECT

_____

_____

_____

_____

Day 2. Why do you look at the speck of sawdust in your brother's eye and pay no attention to the plank in your own eye? (Matt. 7:3)

REFLECT

_____

_____

_____

_____

Day 3. Ask and it will be given to you; seek and you will find; knock and the door will be opened to you. For everyone who asks receives; he who seeks finds; and to him who knocks, the door will be opened (Matt. 7:7–8).

REFLECT

_____

_____

_____

_____

Day 4. So in everything, do to others what you would have them do to you, for this sums up the Law and the Prophets (Matt. 7:12).

REFLECT

_____

_____

_____

_____

Day 5. Enter through the narrow gate. For wide is the gate and broad is the road that leads to destruction, and many enter through it. But small is the gate and narrow the road that leads to life, and only a few find it (Matt. 7:13–14).

REFLECT

_____

_____

_____

_____

Day 6. Use the following space to write any thoughts God has put in your heart and mind during _Session Five_ and your _Reflections_ time this week.

SUMMARY

_____

_____

_____

_____

FALSE CONFIDENCE

MEMORY VERSE: Not everyone who says to me, "Lord, Lord," will enter the kingdom of heaven, but only he who does the will of my Father who is in heaven (Matt. 7:21).

Living in New York in the early 1900s, John Jacob Astor IV was an American millionaire. His $87 million fortune was amassed through real estate and his family's fur-trading empire. After graduating from Harvard, he patented several inventions: a turbine engine, a bicycle brake, and a "vibratory disintegrator" used to produce gas from peat moss. He wrote a science-fiction novel about life on Saturn and Jupiter and financed his own army battalion during the Spanish-American War.

But all his wealth, knowledge, and ingenuity could not save him on the cold disastrous night, April 14, 1912. Astor was a passenger on the RMS *Titanic*.

After an extended honeymoon in Europe and Egypt, Astor and his pregnant wife Madeleine were hurrying back to New York to have their baby in America. The *Titanic* was the quickest and easiest passage back to the States. In the early morning as a ship's officer loaded Madeleine, her maid, and her nurse into lifeboat #4, Astor mentioned Madeleine's "delicate condition" and asked if he could take one of the empty seats in the boat. Even though he was the richest man on board the *Titanic*, the officer refused.

Historians say Astor took it like a gentleman. He lit a cigarette and tossed his gloves to his wife. Days later his partly crushed, soot-stained body was found floating in the Atlantic with $2,500 in his pocket. Experts believe Astor may have been hit by a falling smokestack.

Astor and the other 2,200 people on the boat put their trust and confidence in the "unsinkable" *Titanic* . . . but only a third survived.

In this session we will discuss Jesus's warnings that not all will be saved. We will examine where we place our confidence and ensure our foundation is built on the unsinkable truths of God's Word.

CONNECTING

10 min.

Begin this final session with prayer. Thank God for how he has challenged and encouraged you during this study.

1. This is the last time to connect with your spiritual partner in your small group. What has God been showing you through these sessions about his faithfulness? Have you gained a more full trust in his plan for your life? Check in with each other about the progress you have made in your spiritual growth during this study. Plan whether you will continue in your mentoring relationship outside your Bible study group.

2. Share with the group one thing you have learned during this study that has encouraged you. Also, if you have questions as a result of this study, discuss where you might find the answers.

GROWING

45–50 min.

Jesus concludes his Sermon on the Mount with four warnings.

Read Matthew 7:13–27.

3. What four warnings does Jesus issue in this passage?

4. What is the broad road according to verse 13 and where does it lead?

   What makes the broad road so inviting?

   Why are so many unwilling to follow the narrow road?

5. Jesus is addressing those who have heard his teachings and now must choose how to live. What do you think causes people to pray a prayer for salvation but then avoid doing the things his sermon says to do?

6. Jesus calls false prophets ferocious wolves in sheep's clothing (v. 15). How can we recognize these disguised wolves (vv. 16–20)?

7. What sets a true disciple apart from a false one, according to verse 21?

8. False disciples can do all sorts of things that look like ministry (v. 22), but Jesus declares them insufficient. What about the false disciples do you think is lacking?

   What does this teach us about our own service to the Lord?

9. What is the solid foundation on which we build (v. 24)?

   How do we build upon it?

   Why is it not enough to just believe Jesus's words—why is it essential that we put them into practice?

10. How does doing what Jesus says in the Sermon on the Mount help us to endure life's "storms"?

11. What is one thing from Jesus's Sermon on the Mount that will be especially important for you to practice?

    What help will you need from God and other Christians?

Jesus's Sermon on the Mount demonstrates the inadequacies of a system that seeks righteousness through external behavior without heart transformation. God's standard for righteous living far surpasses any human ability to achieve it and therefore requires a power beyond ourselves. As Jesus concludes his Sermon, he delineates the road that leads to life from the road that leads to destruction. As we yield to the power of God working in and through us as devoted followers of Christ, we are empowered to walk through the narrow gate that leads to life and are assured that the righteousness that God requires is satisfied in Christ.

DEVELOPING   *10 min.*

The Sermon on the Mount describes the character requirements for entering and living in the kingdom of heaven. Everyone who hears Jesus's words and puts them into practice lives as a member of the kingdom where position, authority, and money have no eternal importance. Christ is the model of perfect character. We can't achieve it all at once—we must grow toward it.

12. Prayerfully consider the following actions as a first step toward fulfilling Jesus's commission in your life.

    ☐ Hang a world map in the place where you pray at home. Pray for the world, then each continent, and then each country as the Lord leads you; or pray for the countries printed on your clothing labels as you get dressed every day.

    ☐ Send financial support to a missionary in a foreign country or a world mission organization. Your church will likely have suggestions for who this might be.

    ☐ Sponsor a child through a Christ-centered humanitarian aid organization.

13. If your group still needs to make decisions about continuing to meet after this session, have that discussion now. Talk about what you will study, who will lead, and where and when you will meet.

Review your *Small Group Agreement* and evaluate how well you achieved your goals. Discuss any changes you want to make as you move forward. As your group starts a new study, this is a great time to take on a new role or change roles of service in your group. What new role will you take on? If you are uncertain, maybe your group members have some ideas for you. Remember you aren't making a lifetime commitment to the new role; it will only be for a few weeks. Maybe someone would like to share a role with you if you don't feel ready to serve solo.

SHARING   *10 min.*

Scripture tells that we should always be prepared to give the reason for the hope that we have found in Christ. That's what sharing Christ is all about.

14. During the course of this six-week study, you have made many commitments to share Jesus with the people in your life, either in inviting your believing friends to grow in Christian community or by sharing the gospel in words or actions with unbelievers. Share with the group any highlights that you have experienced as you've stepped out in faith to share with others.

SURRENDERING   *10 min.*

Psalm 106:1 says: "Give thanks to the Lord, for he is good; his love endures forever." It is good to remember and give thanks for what the Lord has done.

15. Look back over the *Prayer and Praise Report*. Are there any answered prayers? Spend a few minutes sharing these in simple, one-sentence prayers of thanks to God. It's important to share your praises along with prayer requests so you can see where God is working in your lives.

16. Close by sharing and praying for your prayer requests. Thank God for what he's done in your group during this study.

Reflections

Get into harmony with God as you spend time with him this week. Read and reflect on the daily verses. Then record your thoughts, insights, or prayers in the *Reflect* sections that follow. On the sixth day record your summary of what God has taught you this week.

Day 1. Enter through the narrow gate. For wide is the gate and broad is the road that leads to destruction, and many enter through it. But small is the gate and narrow the road that leads to life, and only a few find it (Matt. 7:13–14).

REFLECT

_____

_____

_____

_____

Day 2. Likewise every good tree bears good fruit, but a bad tree bears bad fruit. A good tree cannot bear bad fruit, and a bad tree cannot bear good fruit (Matt. 7:17–18).

REFLECT

_____

_____

_____

_____

Day 3. Not everyone who says to me, "Lord, Lord," will enter the kingdom of heaven, but only he who does the will of my Father who is in heaven (Matt. 7:21).

REFLECT

_____

_____

_____

_____

Day 4. Therefore everyone who hears these words of mine and puts them into practice is like a wise man who built his house on the rock (Matt. 7:24).

REFLECT

_____

_____

_____

_____

Day 5. Trust in the LORD with all your heart and lean not on your own understanding; in all your ways acknowledge him, and he will make your paths straight (Prov. 3:5–6).

REFLECT

_____

_____

_____

_____

Day 6. Use the following space to write your prayer of commitment to continue spending time daily in God's Word and prayer.

SUMMARY

_____

_____

_____

_____

APPENDIX

FREQUENTLY ASKED QUESTIONS

What do we do on the first night of our group?
Like all fun things in life—have a party! A "get to know you" coffee, dinner, or dessert is a great way to launch a new study. You may want to review the *Small Group Agreement* and share the names of a few friends you can invite to join you. But most importantly, have fun before your study time begins.

Where do we find new members for our group?
This can be challenging, especially for new groups that have only a few people or for existing groups that lose a few people along the way. Pray with your group and then brainstorm a list of people from work, church, your neighborhood, your children's school, family, the gym, and so forth. Then have each group member invite several of the people on his or her list. Another strategy is to ask church leaders to announce that your group is open to new members.

No matter how you find members, it's vital that you stay on the lookout for new people to join your group. All groups tend to go through healthy attrition—the result of moves, releasing new leaders, ministry opportunities, and so forth—and if the group gets too small, it could be at risk of shutting down. If you and your group stay open, you'll be amazed at the people God sends your way. The next person just might become a friend for life. You never know!

How long will this group meet?
It's up to the group—once you come to the end of this study. Most groups meet weekly for at least their first six months, but every other week can work as well. We recommend that the group meet for the first six months on a weekly basis if possible. This allows for continuity, and if people miss a meeting, they aren't gone for a whole month.

At the end of this study, each group member may decide whether he or she wants to continue on for another study. Some groups launch relationships that last for years, and others are stepping-stones into another group experience. Either way, enjoy the journey.

What if this group is not working for me?

Personality conflicts, life stage differences, geographical distance, level of spiritual maturity, or any number of things can cause you to feel the group doesn't work for you. Relax. Pray for God's direction, and at the end of this study decide whether to continue with this group or find another. You don't buy the first car you look at or marry the first person you date, and the same goes with a group. Don't bail out before the study is finished—God might have something to teach you. Also, don't run from conflict or prejudge people before you have given them a chance. God is still working in you too!

Who is the leader?

Most groups have an official leader. But ideally, the group will mature and members will share the facilitation of meetings. Healthy groups share hosting and leading. This ensures that all members grow, give their unique contribution, and develop their gifts. This study guide and the Holy Spirit can keep things on track even when you share leadership. Christ has promised to be in your midst as you gather. Ultimately, God is your leader each step of the way.

How do we handle the child care needs in our group?

This can be a sensitive issue. We suggest that you empower the group to openly brainstorm solutions. Try one option that works for a while and then adjust over time. Our favorite approach is for adults to share the cost of a babysitter (or two) who can watch the kids in a different part of the house. In this way, parents don't have to be away from their young children all evening. A second option is to use one home for the kids and a second home (close by) for the adults. A third idea is to rotate the adults who provide a lesson or care for the children either in the same home or in another home nearby. This can be an incredible blessing for kids. Finally, the most common idea is to decide that you need to have a night to invest in your spiritual lives individually or as a couple, and make your own arrangements for child care. Whatever the decision, the best approach is to dialogue openly about both the problem and the solution.

SMALL GROUP CALENDAR

Planning and calendaring can help ensure the greatest participation at every meeting. At the end of each meeting, review this calendar. Be sure to include a regular rotation of host homes and leaders, and don't forget birthdays, socials, church events, holidays, and mission/ministry projects.

Date	Lesson	Dessert/Meal	Role

SMALL GROUP AGREEMENT

Our Purpose

To transform our spiritual lives by cultivating our spiritual health in a healthy small group community. In addition, we:

_____

_____

_____

Our Values

Group Attendance	To give priority to the group meeting. We will call or e-mail if we will be late or absent. (Completing the *Small Group Calendar* will minimize this issue.)
Safe Environment	To help create a safe place where people can be heard and feel loved. (Please, no quick answers, snap judgments, or simple fixes.)
Respect Differences	To be gentle and gracious to people with different spiritual maturity, personal opinions, temperaments, or imperfections. We are all works in progress.
Confidentiality	To keep anything that is shared strictly confidential and within the group, and avoid sharing improper information about those outside the group.
Encouragement for Growth	To be not just takers but givers of life. We want to spiritually multiply our lives by serving others with our God-given gifts.
Welcome for Newcomers	To keep an open chair and share Jesus's dream of finding a shepherd for every sheep.
Shared Ownership	To remember that every member is a minister and to ensure that each attender will share a small team role or responsibility over time. (See the *Team Roles*.)
Rotating Hosts/ Leaders and Homes	To encourage different people to host the group in their homes, and to rotate the responsibility of facilitating each meeting. (See the *Small Group Calendar*.)

Our Expectations

- Refreshments/mealtimes _____

- Child care _____

- When we will meet (day of week) _____

- Where we will meet (place) _____

- We will begin at (time) _____ and end at _____

- We will do our best to have some or all of us attend a worship service together. Our primary worship service time will be _____

- Date of this agreement _____

- Date we will review this agreement again _____

- Who (other than the leader) will review this agreement at the end of this study _____

TEAM ROLES

The Bible makes clear that every member, not just the small group leader, is a minister in the body of Christ. In a healthy small group, every member takes on some small role or responsibility. It can be more fun and effective if you team up on these roles.

Review the team roles and responsibilities below, and have each member volunteer for a role or participate on a team. If someone doesn't know where to serve or is holding back, as a group, suggest a team or role. It's best to have one or two people on each team so you have each of the five purposes covered. Serving in even a small capacity will not only help your leader but also will make the group more fun for everyone. Don't hold back. Join a team!

The opportunities below are broken down by the five purposes and then by a *crawl* (beginning), *walk* (intermediate), or *run* (advanced) role. Try to cover at least the crawl and walk roles, and select a role that matches your group, your gifts, and your maturity.

	Team Roles	Team Player(s)
	CONNECTING TEAM (Fellowship and Community Building)	
Crawl:	Host a social event or group activity in the first week or two.	
Walk:	Create a list of uncommitted friends and then invite them to an open house or group social.	
Run:	Plan a twenty-four-hour retreat or weekend getaway for the group.	
	Lead the *Connecting* time each week for the group.	
	GROWING TEAM (Discipleship and Spiritual Growth)	
Crawl:	Coordinate the spiritual partners for the group.	
	Facilitate a three- or four-person discussion circle during the Bible study portion of your meeting.	
	Coordinate the discussion circles.	

Team Roles	Team Player(s)
Walk: Tabulate the *Personal Health Assessment* and *Personal Health Plans* in a summary to let people know how you're doing as a group.	
Encourage personal devotions through group discussions and pairing up with spiritual (accountability) partners.	
Run: Take the group on a prayer walk, or plan a day of solitude, fasting, or personal retreat.	

SERVING TEAM (Discovering Your God-Given Design for Ministry)

Crawl: Ensure that every member finds a group role or team he or she enjoys.	
Walk: Have every member take a gift test and determine your group's gifts.	
Plan a ministry project together.	
Run: Help each member decide on a way to use his or her unique gifts somewhere in the church.	

SHARING TEAM (Sharing and Evangelism)

Crawl: Coordinate the group's *Prayer and Praise Report* of friends and family who don't know Christ.	
Walk: Search for group mission opportunities and plan a cross-cultural group activity.	
Run: Take a small group "vacation" to host a six-week group in your neighborhood or office. Then come back together with your current group.	

SURRENDERING TEAM (Surrendering Your Heart to Worship)

Crawl: Maintain the group's *Pray and Praise Report* or journal.	
Walk: Lead a brief time of worship each week (at the beginning or end of your meeting), either a cappella or using a song from the DVD or a worship CD.	
Run: Plan a unique time of worship through Communion, foot washing, night of prayer, or nature walking.	

PERSONAL HEALTH PLAN

This worksheet could become your single most important feature in this study. On it you can record your personal priorities before the Father. It will help you live a healthy spiritual life, balancing all five of God's purposes.

You will develop your *Personal Health Plan* as you move through the study material in this study guide. At appropriate places during the study, you will be instructed to identify your progress in one or more of the purpose areas (connect, grow, develop, share, surrender) by answering the question associated with the purpose. You may be instructed to discuss with your spiritual partner your progress on one or more steps, and record your progress and the progress of your spiritual partner on the *Progress Report*.

PURPOSE	PLAN
CONNECT	WHO are you connecting with spiritually? **Bill and I will meet weekly by e-mail or phone.**
GROW	WHAT is your next step for growth? **Regular devotions or journaling my prayers 2x/week.**
DEVELOP	WHERE are you serving? **Serving in Children's Ministry** **Go through Gifts Class**
SHARE	WHEN are you shepherding another in Christ? **Shepherding Bill at lunch** **Hosting a starter group in the fall**
SURRENDER	HOW are you surrendering your heart to God? **Help with our teenager** **New job situation**

PURPOSE	PLANNING QUESTION
CONNECT	WHO are you connecting with spiritually?
GROW	WHAT is your next step for growth?
DEVELOP	WHERE are you serving?
SHARE	WHEN are you shepherding another in Christ?
SURRENDER	HOW are you surrendering your heart to God?

DATE	MY PROGRESS	PARTNER'S PROGRESS
3/5	Talked during our group	Figured out our goals together
3/12	Missed our time together	Missed our time together
3/26	Met for coffee and review of my goals	Met for coffee
4/10	E-mailed prayer requests	Praying for partner and group
5/5	Great start on personal journaling	Read Mark 1–6 in one sitting!
5/12	Traveled and not doing well this week	Journaled about Christ as healer
5/26	Back on track	Busy and distracted; asked for prayer
6/1	Need to call Children's Pastor	Scared to lead worship
6/26	Group did a serving project together	Agreed to lead group worship
6/30	Regularly rotating leadership	Led group worship–great job!
7/5	Called Jim to see if he's open to joining our group	Wanted to invite somebody, but didn't
7/12	Preparing to start a group in fall	
7/30	Group prayed for me	Told friend something I'm learning about Christ
8/5	Overwhelmed but encouraged	Absent from group today
8/15	Felt heard and more settled	Issue with wife
8/30	Read book on teens	Glad he took on his fear
9/5	Talked during our group	Figured out our goals together
9/12	Missed our time together	Missed our time together

Progress Report

DATE	MY PROGRESS	PARTNER'S PROGRESS

PERSONAL HEALTH ASSESSMENT

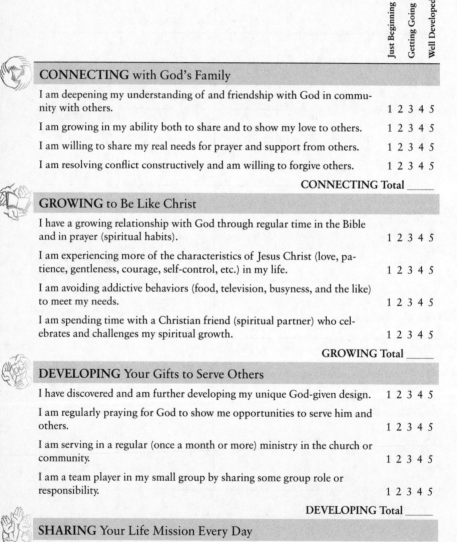

	Just Beginning	Getting Going	Well Developed

CONNECTING with God's Family

I am deepening my understanding of and friendship with God in community with others. 1 2 3 4 5

I am growing in my ability both to share and to show my love to others. 1 2 3 4 5

I am willing to share my real needs for prayer and support from others. 1 2 3 4 5

I am resolving conflict constructively and am willing to forgive others. 1 2 3 4 5

CONNECTING Total _____

GROWING to Be Like Christ

I have a growing relationship with God through regular time in the Bible and in prayer (spiritual habits). 1 2 3 4 5

I am experiencing more of the characteristics of Jesus Christ (love, patience, gentleness, courage, self-control, etc.) in my life. 1 2 3 4 5

I am avoiding addictive behaviors (food, television, busyness, and the like) to meet my needs. 1 2 3 4 5

I am spending time with a Christian friend (spiritual partner) who celebrates and challenges my spiritual growth. 1 2 3 4 5

GROWING Total _____

DEVELOPING Your Gifts to Serve Others

I have discovered and am further developing my unique God-given design. 1 2 3 4 5

I am regularly praying for God to show me opportunities to serve him and others. 1 2 3 4 5

I am serving in a regular (once a month or more) ministry in the church or community. 1 2 3 4 5

I am a team player in my small group by sharing some group role or responsibility. 1 2 3 4 5

DEVELOPING Total _____

SHARING Your Life Mission Every Day

I am cultivating relationships with non-Christians and praying for God to give me natural opportunities to share his love. 1 2 3 4 5

	Just Beginning	Getting Going	Well Developed

I am praying and learning about where God can use me and our group cross-culturally for missions. 　　　　1 2 3 4 5

I am investing my time in another person or group who needs to know Christ. 　　　　1 2 3 4 5

I am regularly inviting unchurched or unconnected friends to my church or small group. 　　　　1 2 3 4 5

SHARING Total _____

SURRENDERING Your Life for God's Pleasure

I am experiencing more of the presence and power of God in my everyday life. 　　　　1 2 3 4 5

I am faithfully attending services and my small group to worship God. 　　　　1 2 3 4 5

I am seeking to please God by surrendering every area of my life (health, decisions, finances, relationships, future, etc.) to him. 　　　　1 2 3 4 5

I am accepting the things I cannot change and becoming increasingly grateful for the life I've been given. 　　　　1 2 3 4 5

SURRENDERING Total _____

	Connecting	Growing	Serving	Sharing	Surrendering	
20	●■ ●■ ●■ ●■	●■ ●■ ●■ ●■	●■ ●■ ●■ ●■	●■ ●■ ●■ ●■	●■ ●■ ●■ ●■	Well Developed
16	●■ ●■ ●■ ●■	●■ ●■ ●■ ●■	●■ ●■ ●■ ●■	●■ ●■ ●■ ●■	●■ ●■ ●■ ●■	Very Good
12	●■ ●■ ●■ ●■	●■ ●■ ●■ ●■	●■ ●■ ●■ ●■	●■ ●■ ●■ ●■	●■ ●■ ●■ ●■	Getting Going
8	●■ ●■ ●■ ●■	●■ ●■ ●■ ●■	●■ ●■ ●■ ●■	●■ ●■ ●■ ●■	●■ ●■ ●■ ●■	Fair
4	●■ ●■ ●■ ●■	●■ ●■ ●■ ●■	●■ ●■ ●■ ●■	●■ ●■ ●■ ●■	●■ ●■ ●■ ●■	Just Beginning

○ Beginning Assessment　　Total _____
□ Ending Assessment　　Total _____

SPIRITUAL GIFTS INVENTORY

A spiritual gift is given to each of us as a means of helping the entire church.

1 Corinthians 12:7 NLT

A spiritual gift is a special ability, given by the Holy Spirit to every believer at their conversion. Although spiritual gifts are given when the Holy Spirit enters new believers, their use and purpose need to be understood and developed as we grow spiritually. A spiritual gift is much like a muscle; the more you use it, the stronger it becomes.

A Few Truths about Spiritual Gifts

1. Only believers have spiritual gifts. 1 Corinthians 2:14
2. You can't earn or work for a spiritual gift. Ephesians 4:7
3. The Holy Spirit decides what gifts I get. 1 Corinthians 12:11
4. I am to develop the gifts God gives me. Romans 11:29; 2 Timothy 1:6
5. It's a sin to waste the gifts God gave me. 1 Corinthians 4:1–2; Matthew 25:14–30
6. Using my gifts honors God and expands me. John 15:8

Gifts Inventory

God wants us to know what spiritual gift(s) he has given us. One person can have many gifts. The goal is to find the areas in which the Holy Spirit seems to have supernaturally empowered our service to others. These gifts are to be used to minister to others and build up the body of Christ.

There are four main lists of gifts found in the Bible in Romans 12:3–8; 1 Corinthians 12:1–11, 27–31; Ephesians 4:11–12; and 1 Peter 4:9–11. There are other passages that mention or illustrate gifts not included in these lists. As you read through this list, prayerfully consider whether the biblical definition describes you. Remember, you can have more than one gift, but everyone has at least one.

ADMINISTRATION (Organization)—1 Corinthians 12

This is the ability to recognize the gifts of others and recruit them to a ministry. It is the ability to organize and manage people, resources, and time for effective ministry.

APOSTLE—1 Corinthians 12

This is the ability to start new churches/ventures and oversee their development.

DISCERNMENT—1 Corinthians 12

This is the ability to distinguish between the spirit of truth and the spirit of error; to detect inconsistencies in another's life and confront in love.

ENCOURAGEMENT (Exhortation)—Romans 12

This is the ability to motivate God's people to apply and act on biblical principles, especially when they are discouraged or wavering in their faith. It is also the ability to bring out the best in others and challenge them to develop their potential.

EVANGELISM—Ephesians 4

This is the ability to communicate the gospel of Jesus Christ to unbelievers in a positive, nonthreatening way and to sense opportunities to share Christ and lead people to respond with faith.

FAITH—1 Corinthians 12

This is the ability to trust God for what cannot be seen and to act on God's promise, regardless of what the circumstances indicate. This includes a willingness to risk failure in pursuit of a God-given vision, expecting God to handle the obstacles.

GIVING—Romans 12

This is the ability to generously contribute material resources and/or money beyond the 10 percent tithe so that the church may grow and be strengthened. It includes the ability to manage money so it may be given to support the ministry of others.

HOSPITALITY—1 Peter 4:9–10

This is the ability to make others, especially strangers, feel warmly welcomed, accepted, and comfortable in the church family and the ability to coordinate factors that promote fellowship.

LEADERSHIP—Romans 12

This is the ability to clarify and communicate the purpose and direction ("vision") of a ministry in a way that attracts others to get involved, including the ability to motivate others, by example, to work together in accomplishing a ministry goal.

MERCY—Romans 12

This is the ability to manifest practical, compassionate, cheerful love toward suffering members of the body of Christ.

PASTORING (Shepherding)—Ephesians 4

This is the ability to care for the spiritual needs of a group of believers and equip them for ministry. It is also the ability to nurture a small group in spiritual growth and assume responsibility for their welfare.

PREACHING—Romans 12

This is the ability to publicly communicate God's Word in an inspired way that convinces unbelievers and both challenges and comforts believers.

SERVICE—Romans 12

This is the ability to recognize unmet needs in the church family, and take the initiative to provide practical assistance quickly, cheerfully, and without a need for recognition.

TEACHING—Ephesians 4

This is the ability to educate God's people by clearly explaining and applying the Bible in a way that causes them to learn; it is the ability to equip and train other believers for ministry.

WISDOM—1 Corinthians 12

This is the ability to understand God's perspective on life situations and share those insights in a simple, understandable way.

SERVING COMMUNION

Churches vary in their treatment of *Communion* (or *The Lord's Supper*). We offer one simple form by which a small group can share this experience together. You can adapt this as necessary, or omit it from your group altogether, depending on your church's beliefs.

Steps in Serving Communion

1. Open by sharing about God's love, forgiveness, grace, mercy, commitment, tenderheartedness, faithfulness, etc., out of your personal journey (connect with the stories of those in the room).
2. Read the passage: "And he took bread, gave thanks and broke it, and gave it to them, saying, 'This is my body given for you; do this in remembrance of me'" (Luke 22:19).
3. Pray and pass the bread around the circle.
4. When everyone has been served, remind them that this represents Jesus's broken body on their behalf. Simply state, "Jesus said, 'Do this in remembrance of me' (Luke 22:19). Let us eat together," and eat the bread as a group.
5. Then read the rest of the passage: "In the same way, after the supper he took the cup, saying, 'This cup is the new covenant in my blood, which is poured out for you'" (Luke 22:20).
6. Pray and serve the cups, either by passing a small tray, serving them individually, or having members pick up a cup from the table.
7. When everyone has been served, remind them the juice represents Christ's blood shed for them, then simply state, "Take and drink in remembrance of him. Let us drink together."
8. Finish by singing a simple song, listening to a praise song, or having a time of prayer in thanks to God.

Communion passages: Matthew 26:26–29; Mark 14:22–25; Luke 22:14–20; 1 Corinthians 10:16–21; 11:17–34

PERFORMING A FOOTWASHING

Scripture: John 13:1–17. Jesus makes it quite clear to his disciples that his position as the Father's Son includes being a servant rather than being one of power and glory only.

The Purpose of Footwashing

To properly understand the scene and the intention of Jesus, we must realize that the washing of feet was the duty of slaves and indeed of non-Jewish rather than Jewish slaves. Jesus placed himself in the position of a servant. He displayed to the disciples self-sacrifice and love. In view of his majesty, only the symbolic position of a slave was adequate to open their eyes and keep them from lofty illusions. The point of footwashing, then, is to correct the attitude that Jesus discerned in the disciples. It constitutes the permanent basis for mutual service, service in your group and for the community around you, which is laid on all Christians.

When to Implement

There are three primary places we would recommend you insert a footwashing:

- during a break in the *Surrendering* section of your group
- during a break in the *Growing* section of your group
- at the closing of your group

A special time of prayer for each person as he or she gets his or her feet washed can be added to the footwashing time.

SURRENDERING AT THE CROSS

Surrendering everything to God is one of the most challenging aspects of following Jesus. It involves a relationship built on trust and faith. Each of us is in a different place on our spiritual journey. Some of us have known the Lord for many years, some are new in our faith, and some may still be checking God out. Regardless, we all have things that we still want control over—things we don't want to give to God because we don't know what he will do with them. These things are truly more important to us than God is—they have become our god.

We need to understand that God wants us to be completely devoted to him. If we truly love God with all our heart, soul, strength, and mind (Luke 10:27), we will be willing to give him everything.

Steps in Surrendering at the Cross

1. You will need some small pieces of paper and pens or pencils for people to write down the things they want to sacrifice/surrender to God.
2. If you have a wooden cross, hammers, and nails, you can have the members nail their sacrifices to the cross. If you don't have a wooden cross, get creative. Think of another way to symbolically relinquish the sacrifices to God. You might use a fireplace to burn them in the fire as an offering to the Lord. The point is giving to the Lord whatever hinders your relationship with him.
3. Create an atmosphere conducive to quiet reflection and prayer. Whatever this quiet atmosphere looks like for your group, do the best you can to create a peaceful time to meet with God.
4. Once you are settled, prayerfully think about the points below. Let the words and thoughts draw you into a heart-to-heart connection with your Lord Jesus Christ.

    ☐ **Worship him.** Ask God to change your viewpoint so you can worship him through a surrendered spirit.

93

☐ **Humble yourself.** Surrender doesn't happen without humility. James 4:6–7 says, "'God opposes the proud but gives grace to the humble.' Submit yourselves, then, to God."

☐ **Surrender your mind, will, and emotions.** This is often the toughest part of surrendering. What do you sense God urging you to give him so you can have the kind of intimacy he desires with you? Our hearts yearn for this kind of connection with him; let go of the things that stand between you.

☐ **Write out your prayer.** Write out your prayer of sacrifice and surrender to the Lord. This may be an attitude, a fear, a person, a job, a possession—anything that God reveals is a hindrance to your relationship with him.

5. After writing out your sacrifice, take it to the cross and offer it to the Lord. Nail your sacrifice to the cross, or burn it as a sacrifice in the fire.

6. Close by singing, praying together, or taking communion. Make this time as short or as long as seems appropriate for your group.

Surrendering to God is life-changing and liberating. God desires that we be overcomers! First John 4:4 says, "You, dear children, are from God and have overcome . . . because the one who is in you is greater than the one who is in the world."

PRAYER AND PRAISE REPORT

Briefly share your prayer requests with the large group, making notations below. Then gather in small groups of two to four to pray for each other.

SESSION 1

Prayer Requests

_____

_____

_____

_____

_____

Praise Reports

_____

_____

_____

_____

SESSION 2

Prayer Requests

_____

_____

_____

_____

_____

Praise Reports

_____

_____

_____

_____

_____

SESSION 3

Prayer Requests

_____

_____

_____

_____

_____

Praise Reports

_____

_____

_____

_____

_____

SESSION 4

Prayer Requests

_____

_____

_____

_____

_____

Praise Reports

_____

_____

_____

_____

_____

SESSION 5

Prayer Requests

_____

_____

_____

_____

_____

Praise Reports

_____

_____

_____

_____

_____

SESSION 6

Prayer Requests

_____
_____
_____
_____
_____

Praise Reports

_____
_____
_____
_____
_____

JOURNALING 101

Henri Nouwen says effective and lasting ministry *for* God grows out of a quiet place alone *with* God. This is why journaling is so important.

The greatest adventure of our lives is found in the daily pursuit of knowing, growing in, serving, sharing, and worshiping Christ forever. This is the essence of a purposeful life: to see all these biblical purposes fully formed and balanced in our lives. Only then are we "complete in Christ" (Col. 1:28 NASB).

David poured his heart out to God by writing psalms. The book of Psalms contains many of his honest conversations with God in written form, including expressions of every imaginable emotion on every aspect of his life. Like David, we encourage you to select a strategy to integrate God's Word and journaling into your devotional time. Use any of the following resources:

- Bible
- Bible reading plan
- Devotional
- Topical Bible study plan

Before and after you read a portion of God's Word, speak to God in honest reflection in the form of a written prayer. You may begin this time by simply finishing the sentence "Father, . . . ," "Yesterday, Lord, . . . ," or "Thank you, God, for . . ." Share with him where you are at the present moment; express your hurts, disappointments, frustrations, blessings, victories, and gratefulness. Whatever you do with your journal, make a plan that fits you, so you'll have a positive experience. Consider sharing highlights of your progress and experiences with some or all of your group members, especially your spiritual partner. You may find they want to join and even encourage you in this journey. Most of all, enjoy the ride and cultivate a more authentic, growing walk with God.

HOW TO HAVE A QUIET TIME

Every relationship takes time to develop. You have to spend time with someone to take a relationship deeper. It's no different with our relationship with the Lord. A quiet time is time alone with the Lord. Each day we need to set aside time with him for Bible reading and prayer. As Christians, our primary goal is to become "conformed to the likeness of [God's] Son" (Rom. 8:29). "But one who looks intently at the perfect law, the law of liberty, and abides by it, not having become a forgetful hearer but an effectual doer, this man will be blessed in what he does" (James 1:25 NASB).

Five reasons to have a quiet time with God are:

- We need nourishment from God's Word to grow.
- We need to draw close to God.
- The Word is our best defense against sin.
- We need to be corrected when we sin.
- We need encouragement and comfort.

Three elements of an effective quiet time:

- Bible reading
- Prayer time
- Journaling and Bible note-taking

Tips for a meaningful quiet time:

- Recognize that you were created to be in relationship with God and he desires to spend time with you.
- Set a consistent time each day to spend with Jesus. Early morning or evening, children's nap times, and lunch hours are typical

times. If your quiet time is scheduled, you are much more likely to keep it.

- Get free from distractions (family members, telephone, TV, e-mail, etc.). Try to eliminate all sounds such as music that might keep you from hearing from God.
- If you miss a quiet time, don't beat yourself up over it. Realize that you got distracted or chose not to have that time that day. Just begin again. The longer you wait, the harder it is to make it a regular habit.
- If your quiet time is dry, difficult, or monotonous, try something new. Consider changing your Bible version, changing your location, listening to the Bible on tape, or changing your routine of reading and praying. Enjoy your time with God.

Beginning your quiet time:

- Pick a quiet place that works for you to meet the Lord.
- Have your Bible, notebook, and pen with you.
- Start with prayer by asking God to
  o meet with you
  o prevent distractions
  o reveal his Word for you today
  o bring comfort and clarification for your life
- Read the passage of Scripture you have selected for the day.
- Write down some of your observations from your Bible reading by answering the following two questions:
  o What does the passage say generally (what is it teaching me)?
  o What does the passage say to me personally (what should I do specifically)?
- Record any insights, thoughts, fears, concerns, praises, or feelings you have from your time with God.
- Respond to God in prayer in the following ways:
  o Praise and thanksgiving—"I praise you, God, for . . ."
  o Repentance and confession—"I confess my sin of . . ."
  o Guidance—"Lord, lead me today by . . ."
  o Obedience—"I will obey you in . . ."

LEADING FOR THE FIRST TIME
LEADERSHIP 101

Sweaty palms are a healthy sign. The Bible says God is gracious to the humble. Remember who is in control; the time to worry is when you're *not* worried. Those who are soft in heart (and sweaty palmed) are those whom God is sure to speak through.

Seek support. Ask your leader, co-leader, or close friend to pray for you and prepare with you before the session. Walking through the study will help you anticipate potentially difficult questions and discussion topics.

Bring your uniqueness to the study. Lean into who you are and how God wants you to uniquely lead the study.

Prepare. Prepare. Prepare. Go through the session several times. If you are using the DVD, listen to the teaching segment and *Leader Lifter*. Consider writing in a journal or fasting for a day to prepare yourself for what God wants to do.

Don't wait until the last minute to prepare.

Ask for feedback so you can grow. Perhaps in an e-mail or on cards handed out at the study, have everyone write down three things you did well and one thing you could improve on. Don't get defensive, but show an openness to learn and grow.

Prayerfully consider launching a new group. This doesn't need to happen overnight, but God's heart is for this to happen over time. Not all Christians are called to be leaders or teachers, but we are all called to be "shepherds" of a few someday.

Share with your group what God is doing in your heart. God is searching for those whose hearts are fully his. Share your trials and victories. We promise that people will relate.

Prayerfully consider whom you would like to pass the baton to next week. It's only fair. God is ready for the next member of your group to go on the faith journey you just traveled. Make it fun, and expect God to do the rest.

Congratulations! You have responded to the call to help shepherd Jesus's flock. There are few other tasks in the family of God that surpass the contribution you will be making. We have provided you several ways to prepare for this role. Between the *Read Me First*, these *Leader's Notes*, and the *Watch This First* and *Leader Lifter* segments on the optional *Deepening Life Together: Sermon on the Mount* Video Teaching DVD, you'll have all you need to do a great job of leading your group. Just don't forget, you are not alone. God knew that you would be asked to lead this group and he won't let you down. In Hebrews 13:5b God promises us, "Never will I leave you; never will I forsake you."

Your role as leader is to create a safe, warm environment for your group. As a leader, your most important job is to create an atmosphere where people are willing to talk honestly about what the topics discussed in this study have to do with them. Be available before people arrive so you can greet them at the door. People are naturally nervous at a new group, so a hug or handshake can help put them at ease. Before you start leading your group, a little preparation will give you confidence. Review the *Read Me First* at the front of your study guide so you'll understand the purpose of each section, enabling you to help your group understand it as well.

If you're new to leading a group, congratulations and thank you; this will be a life-changing experience for you also. We have provided these *Leader's Notes* to help new leaders begin well.

It's important in your first meeting to make sure group members understand that things shared personally and in prayer must remain confidential. Also, be careful not to dominate the group discussion, but facilitate it and encourage others to join in and share. And lastly, have fun.

Take a moment at the beginning of your first meeting to orient the group to one principle that undergirds this study: A healthy small group balances the purposes of the church. Most small groups emphasize Bible study, fellowship, and prayer. But God has called us to reach out to others as well. He wants us to do what Jesus teaches, not just learn about it.

Preparing for each meeting ahead of time. Take the time to review the session, the *Leader's Notes*, and the optional *Leader Lifter* for the session before each session. Also write down your answers to each question. Pay special attention to exercises that ask group members to *do* something. These exercises will help your group live out what the Bible teaches, not just talk about it. Be sure you understand how the exercises work, and bring any supplies you might need, such as paper or pens. Pray for your group members by name at least once between sessions and before each session. Use the *Prayer and Praise Report* so you will remember their prayer requests. Ask God to use your time together to touch the heart of every person. Expect God to give you the opportunity to talk with those he wants you to encourage or challenge in a special way.

Don't try to go it alone. Pray for God to help you. Ask other members of your group to help by taking on some small role. In the *Appendix* you'll find the *Team Roles* pages with some suggestions to get people involved. Leading is more rewarding if you give group members opportunities to help. Besides, helping group members discover their individual gifts for serving or even leading the group will bless all of you.

Consider asking a few people to come early to help set up, pray, and introduce newcomers to others. Even if everyone is new, they don't know that yet and may be shy when they arrive. You might give people roles like setting up name tags or handing out drinks. This could be a great way to spot a co-leader.

Subgrouping. If your group has more than seven people, break into discussion groups of three to four people for the *Growing* and *Surrendering* sections each week. People will connect more with the study and each other when they have more opportunity to participate. Smaller discussion circles encourage quieter people to talk more and tend to minimize the effects of more vocal or dominant members. Also, people who are unaccustomed to praying aloud will feel more comfortable praying within a smaller group of people. Share prayer requests in the larger group and then break into smaller groups to pray for each other. People are more willing to pray in small circles if they know that the whole group will hear all the prayer requests.

Memorizing Scripture. At the start of each session you will find a memory verse—a verse for the group to memorize each week. Encourage your group members to do this. Memorizing God's Word is both directed and celebrated throughout the Bible, either explicitly ("Your word I have hidden in my heart, that I might not sin against You" [Ps. 119:11 NKJV]), or implicitly, as in the example of our Lord ("He departed to the mountain to pray" [Mark 6:46 NKJV]).

Anyone who has memorized Scripture can confirm the amazing spiritual benefits that result from this practice. Don't miss out on the opportunity to encourage your group to grow in the knowledge of God's Word through Scripture memorization.

Reflections. We've provided opportunity for a personal time with God using the *Reflections* at the end of each session. Don't press seekers to do this, but just remind the group that every believer should have a plan for personal time with God.

Inviting new people. Cast the vision, as Jesus did, to be inclusive, not exclusive. Ask everyone to prayerfully think of people who would enjoy or benefit from a group like this—then invite them. The beginning of a new study is a great time to welcome a few people into your circle. Don't worry about ending up with too many people—you can always have one discussion circle in the living room and another in the dining room.

For Deeper Study (Optional). We have included a *For Deeper Study* section in most sessions. *For Deeper Study* provides additional passages for individual study on the topic of each session. If your group likes to do deeper Bible study, consider having members study the *For Deeper Study* passages for homework. Then, during the *Growing* portion of your meeting, you can share the high points of what you've learned.

LEADER'S NOTES

SESSIONS

Session One People Who Change the World

Connecting

1. Allow each participant to introduce themselves to the group. Whether your group is new or ongoing, there may be new people in the group who don't yet have an established relationship with the group. New groups will need to invest more time building relationships with each other.

2. A very important item in this first session is the *Small Group Agreement*. An agreement helps clarify your group's priorities and cast new vision for what the group can become. You can find this in the *Appendix* of this study guide. We've found that groups that talk about these values up front and commit to an agreement benefit significantly. They work through conflicts long before people get to the point of frustration, so there's a lot less pain.

   Take some time to review this agreement before your meeting. Then during your meeting, read the agreement aloud to the entire group. If some people have concerns about a specific item or the agreement as a whole, be sensitive to their concerns. Explain that tens of thousands of groups use agreements like this one as a simple tool for building trust and group health over time.

   As part of this discussion, we recommend talking about shared ownership of the group. It's important that each member have a role. See *Team Roles*. This is a great tool to get this important practice launched in your group.

   Also, you will find a *Small Group Calendar* in the *Appendix* for use in planning your group meetings and roles. Take a look at the calendar prior to your first meeting and point it out to the group so that each person can note when and where the group will meet, who will bring snacks, any important upcoming events (birthdays, anniversaries), etc.

3. Ask for volunteers to answer the introductory question after the group members have had an opportunity to introduce themselves and review the *Small Group Agreement*.

Growing

Have someone read Bible passages aloud. It's a good idea to ask ahead of time, because not everyone is comfortable reading aloud in public.

4. The word "blessed" in the context of Matthew 5:3–11 means "happy or privileged" and conveys the idea of being especially favored by God. Jesus makes a clear delineation between worldly happiness and the blessedness of God's kingdom in his use of paradox. Worldly happiness is not found in poverty, humility, and self-sacrifice, but in perceived wealth, vanity, and abundance, which are temporary and ultimately prove empty.

5. See the chart below.

Blessed are . . .	How does this apply to our lives?	How do we fall short?
The poor in spirit (v. 3)	Deep humility. Awareness of spiritual bankruptcy, of having no resources for self-help.	We try to be self-sufficient, not trusting God with everything. We are proud.
Those who mourn (v. 4)	Profound sorrow over sin and loss suffered for the sake of following Jesus.	We lack repentance over certain sins in our life. We are self-satisfied and unmoved by our faith.
The meek (v. 5)	Gentleness and care toward others, as opposed to aggression, domination, or apathy.	We behave with aggression toward others, controlling or forceful.
Those who hunger and thirst for righteousness (v. 6)	Yearning for and seeking God's standards for right living to prevail in one's own heart and behavior, in one's community, and around the globe.	We believe we are "good people." We feel that we've got our acts together. We think we are better than others, especially those who don't know Jesus.
The merciful (v. 7)	Sharing in the afflictions of others. Offering forgiveness and compassion.	We remain unsympathetic to the needs of our neighbors or communities.
The pure in heart (v. 8)	Honesty with God. Attention to the motives and desires that drive behavior, rather than simply external conformity.	We behave dishonorably. We "hide" our sins from God and others. We behave like Christians at church and not at other times.
The peacemakers (v. 9)	Promoting peace with God, in personal relationships, and among larger groups of people.	We are self-seeking, needing to be right or justified in discussions. Our relationships are full of strife.

Those per-secuted because of righteousness (vv. 10–11)	Suffering for standing up for God's standards of righteousness.	We have constantly shifting ideologies.

7. Each of these blessings is an act of God's divine grace and mercy and can't be achieved by our own accomplishments. They don't represent earthly riches or rewards, but spiritual blessings, such as inclusion in the kingdom of heaven and forgiveness of sin. Some of them we receive immediately when we become children of God, but others we have to wait for with patient hope.

8. Our hearts' desire should be righteousness in God's eyes. This includes all the attitudes represented in the Beatitudes, such as deep humility, repentance for our sin, compassion toward others, pure motives, and integrity in all circumstances. Our appetites for righteousness will be filled only by a daily portion of grace to act according to the will of our Lord.

9. Some substitutions are achieving success in the workplace, acquisition of material possessions or wealth, and recreation; always wanting to "be the best" and "have the best" in the eyes of the world.

    We need the grace of God through the power of the Holy Spirit, and we also need the willingness to submit to that grace. We need to endure the discomfort of facing the things we hunger for and confessing those things to God. Sometimes other people can be very helpful. God wants to help us do what we can't do on our own.

10. The whole Bible is about God's plan to reconcile us to him—to make our relationships whole again. Jesus is teaching about reconciliation when he says blessed are the peacemakers. We should be about bringing reconcilia-tion, or making peace, between those who are in conflict.

11. Possible answers include ridicule for living uprightly, personal attack on political or social ideologies, and rebellion by children who live in opposi-tion to family values.

Developing

This section enables you to help the group see the importance of devel-oping their abilities for service to God.

14. The intent of this question is to encourage group members to set aside some time to spend with God in prayer and his Word at home each day throughout the week. Read through this section and be prepared to help the group understand how important it is to fill our minds with the Word

of God. If people already have a good Bible reading plan and commitment, that is great, but you may have people who struggle to stay in the Word daily. Sometimes beginning with a simple commitment to a short daily reading can start a habit that changes a life. The *Reflections* pages at the end of each session include verses that were either talked about in the session or support the teaching of the session. They are very short readings with a few lines to encourage people to write down their thoughts. Remind the group about these *Reflections* each week after the *Surrendering* section. Encourage the group to see the importance of making time to connect with God a priority in their life. Encourage everyone to commit to a next step in prayer, Bible reading, or meditation on the Word.

Sharing

Jesus wants all of his disciples to help outsiders connect with him, to know him personally. This section should provide an opportunity to go beyond Bible study to biblical living.

16. Encourage the group to observe their interactions during the coming week with the intention of using these observations next week in evaluating the people that God has placed in their lives that he might want them to share with or invite to small group.

Surrendering

God is most pleased by a heart that is fully his. Each session will provide group members a chance to surrender their hearts to God in prayer and worship. Group prayer requests and prayer time should be included every week.

18. Encourage group members to use the *Reflections* verses in their daily quiet time throughout the week. This will move them closer to God while reinforcing the lesson of this session through related Scripture.

19. As you move to a time of sharing prayer requests, be sure to remind the group of the importance of confidentiality and keeping what is shared in the group within the group. Everyone must feel that the personal things they share will be kept confident if you are to have safety and bonding among group members.

For Deeper Study

We have included an optional *For Deeper Study* section in most sessions. *For Deeper Study* provides additional passages for individual study on the topic of each session. If your group likes to do deeper Bible study, consider having members study the *For Deeper Study* passages at home between meetings.

Session Two How Good Is Good Enough?

Connecting

2. Allow everyone to answer this icebreaker question.

Growing

3. The Law and Prophets refers to Old Testament Scripture. Jesus did not come to abolish the law or to remove even the smallest detail from it. Jesus fulfills the law in that he brings it to completion by ushering in the kingdom of God. We must observe the law as the Holy Spirit empowers us from the inside out.

4. Jesus is referring to the righteousness we can receive freely through him and live out in the power of the Holy Spirit. First, God "imputes" righteousness to us—he treats us as if we live the Sermon on the Mount perfectly, even though we don't. Second, he increasingly instills righteousness in us—he empowers us through his Spirit to live by the Sermon on the Mount and the rest of his commands, if we cooperate with him. No one can achieve righteousness through his or her own effort; therefore, none will enter the kingdom of heaven (receive salvation) without receiving God's grace through faith in Jesus. But as we'll see, the righteousness Jesus calls for is higher than the righteousness the Pharisees called for, because they believed righteous acts like avoiding murder and adultery were enough, while Jesus insisted that heart-level righteousness—confronting the sinful desires within us—was also essential. This is what the Holy Spirit wants to do in us.

6. While the law prohibited murder, contemptuous anger or abusive language is murder on the level of heart attitude and, as the motive for murder, will be judged as murder. We may be able to stop ourselves short of the violent act or abusive words, but controlling the aggressive impulse requires much deeper repentance in the heart.

7. Acts of reconciliation resolve anger before it becomes destructive. A spontaneous emotion is not a sin, but an emotion nursed in the heart—along with contemptuous thoughts about the other person and desires for revenge—is sin. We need to pay attention to our emotions and deal with them before they lead to sin (or confess and repent of them as soon as they do lead to sin).

8. Entertaining the desire for sexual intimacy with someone (except for one's spouse) is lust. More generally, any thought that leads your mind to think inappropriately is adultery of the heart and will be judged just like adultery.

9. Jesus is not advocating self-mutilation in order to prevent sin. Plucking out our eyes will not cure lust. The point he is making is that it would be better to lose part of our bodies than to live with the eternal consequences of sin. We must be willing to make painful sacrifices in order to cast our sins as far from us as possible. In a practical sense, we might avoid mental input that feeds lust (provocative photographs, sexually explicit films, TV, and magazines, steamy romance novels, etc.).

10. In a culture where one often gave one's word rather than signing a contract, the rabbis handled oaths in varying degrees of seriousness. Jesus says you should not need to back up your word with an oath, but rather should speak and act with absolute integrity in all matters. Careless oaths in our everyday speech cause us to be dishonest when we don't follow through, like when we promise to pray for someone and then forget. We must become people of integrity, speaking honestly and keeping our word. When we say we will do something, we must do it. If we cannot, then we must say so. (Although verse 22 relates to cursing at others, this passage is not about cursing. Paul rebukes cursing in Eph. 4:29.)

11. Jesus spoke to people who were harshly oppressed by Roman soldiers and rich overlords. He lived in violent times, and he was no impractical idealist. Yet the voice of our hearts often responds to his teaching with words like, "That sounds nice, but if I did that at work, people would walk all over me." It's important for us to notice the ways in which we tend to resist Jesus's teaching.

12. Jesus had worse enemies than we have, and he knew how hard it was to actively seek the good of those who treat us with malice. He isn't asking us to like everyone, but he is asking us to uproot the vengefulness and selfishness inside us that make us want retribution. Above all, he isn't asking for pretense but for inner changes that make loving behavior coherent. Prayer is one of the most practical ways that we express love. It changes our hearts toward our enemies as we invite God to work in their lives.

13. Jesus is interested in the condition of our hearts—the motives or attitudes that lead us to sin—and wants us to deal with them before they manifest outwardly. He reveals that God's heart loves even those who don't love him, that God cares about integrity and keeps his commitments, that he values sexual purity and the marriage covenant, and that the kind of malice that leads to verbal abuse and murder is utterly foreign to him.

14. The only way to become fully developed in this way is to admit we are far from fully developed and are incapable of becoming morally mature on our

own. We need God's forgiveness through Christ. We must also be honest with ourselves and him about the specific ways we fall short of living by his teaching, and seek his grace for the transformation of our hearts in surrender to him. We need to immerse ourselves in the way he thinks so that his ways overwrite our old habits. Moral perfection isn't a standard for earning our way into God's kingdom. Rather it is the Holy Spirit's goal for those who are already in God's kingdom.

Developing

15. For many, spiritual partners will be a new idea. We highly encourage you to try pairs for this study. It's so hard to start a spiritual practice like prayer or consistent Bible reading with no support. A friend makes a huge difference. As leader, you may want to prayerfully decide who would be a good match with whom. Remind people that this partnership isn't forever; it's just for a few weeks. Be sure to have extra copies of the *Personal Health Plan* available at this meeting in case you need to have a group of three spiritual partners. It is a good idea for you to look over the *Personal Health Plan* before the meeting so you can help people understand how to use it.

    Instruct your group members to enlist a spiritual partner by asking them to pair up with someone in the group (we suggest that men partner with men and women with women) and turn to the *Personal Health Plan*.

    Ask the group to complete the instructions for the WHO and WHAT questions on the *Personal Health Plan*. Your group has now begun to address two of God's purposes for their lives!

    You can see that the *Personal Health Plan* contains space to record the ups and downs and progress each week in the column labeled "My Progress." When partners check in each week, they can record their partner's progress in the goal he or she chose in the "Partner's Progress" column on this chart. In the *Appendix*, you'll find a *Sample Personal Health Plan* filled in as an example.

    The WHERE, WHEN, and HOW questions on the *Personal Health Plan* will be addressed in future sessions of the study.

16. Encourage the group to plan a social or potluck outside of small group time. Socializing together provides the group an opportunity to build stronger relationships between individual members as well as allows time for celebrating what God is doing through this small group Bible study.

Sharing

17. A *Circles of Life* diagram is provided for you and the group to use to help you identify people who need a connection to Christian community. Encourage the group to commit to praying for God's guidance and an opportunity to reach out to each person in their *Circles of Life*.

We encourage this outward focus for your group, because groups that become too inwardly focused tend to become unhealthy over time. People naturally gravitate toward feeding themselves through Bible study, prayer, and social time, so it's usually up to the leader to push them to consider how this inward nourishment can overflow into outward concern for others. Never forget: Jesus came to seek and save the lost and to find a shepherd for every sheep.

Talk to the group about the importance of inviting people; remind them that healthy small groups make a habit of inviting friends, neighbors, unconnected church members, co-workers, etc., to join their groups or join them at a weekend church service. When people get connected to a group of new friends, they often join the church.

Some groups are happy with the people they already have in the group and they don't really want to grow larger. Some fear that newcomers will interrupt the intimacy that members have built over time. However, groups generally gain strength with the infusion of new people. It's like a river of living water flowing into a stagnant pond. Some groups remain permanently open, while others open periodically, such as at the beginning and end of a study. If your circle becomes too large for easy face-to-face conversations, you can simply form a second or third discussion circle in another room in your home.

Surrendering

19. Last week we talked briefly about incorporating *Reflections* into the group members' daily time with God. Some people don't yet have an established quiet time. With this in mind, engage a discussion within the group about the importance of making daily time with God a priority. Talk about potential obstacles and practical ideas for how to overcome them. Encourage group members to refer to *How to Have a Quiet Time* in the *Appendix* for ideas. The *Reflections* verses could serve as a springboard for drawing near to God. So don't forget these are a valuable resource for your group.

20. Be sure to remind the group of the importance of confidentiality and keeping what is shared in the group within the group. Use the *Prayer and Praise Report* in the *Appendix* to record your prayer requests.

Session Three An Audience of One

Connecting

1. Encourage group members to take time to complete the *Personal Health Assessment* and pair up with their spiritual partner to discuss one thing that is going well and one thing that needs work. Participants should not

be asked to share any aspect of this assessment in the large group if they don't want to.

Growing

3. We should not act out of pride or a need to impress others. These should be acts of worship motivated by love for God. Jesus's concern is with the condition of the heart.

4. If our acts of righteousness are done before others, then our reward will be their admiration. We cannot expect to be rewarded by both God and people. Our acts of righteousness are for God alone.

5. Jesus again uses hyperbole to illustrate a point: Giving should be unpretentious. Giving that pleases the Lord isn't done to impress ourselves either. It shouldn't puff up our pride in being so generous.

6. Jesus isn't forbidding us to pray aloud or with others present. (The Scriptures are full of references to the power of group prayer.) His point is that prayer shouldn't be a performance for others but an intimate conversation with God. It's easier to let go of the perceived pressure to pray eloquently before others if we're alone with God. Prayer that we offer to God in our most secret places tends to be unrefined and genuine—from our heart to the heart of God. This is the type of prayer that is honoring to the Father.

7. The pagans recited lists of gods, hoping to mention the right one (name-dropping), often in attempt to say the magic words to get the god to do what one wanted. It wasn't a conversation between persons. There was no listening involved, and love was largely immaterial. By contrast, we should pray simply and genuinely. Attitude matters more than eloquence. Christians tend to use a lot of "filler" words when praying—words to fill the silent gaps—especially in groups. If we are mindful of our words and offer simple petitions to the Lord from our hearts, then we'll do less of this. We talk openly and mindfully with others, and we should do the same with God.

8. Prayer expresses our dependence upon God to supply our needs, and our thankfulness to him for doing so as well.

9. Prayer according to this model demonstrates a willingness to submit freely and obediently to God's will. It expresses trusting dependence on him to provide our daily needs—both to care for us physically and to nourish us spiritually. It communicates our continual reliance on him to free us from bondage to sin and protect us from danger. This is a prayer that demonstrates a heart truly surrendered to God and his purposes.

10. Our salvation from sin does not depend on our forgiveness of others, but our forgiveness for others overflows from the great realization that God has

forgiven us. It is evidence of our saving faith in Christ. We cannot profess faith in Christ and testify to his forgiveness for our sins, and still harbor animosity toward others. As we forgive others, we testify to the forgiveness which we have received. Forgiveness doesn't mean forgetting. Nor does it mean saying the wrong was OK (God doesn't say our sins are OK either). It means letting go of bitterness, resentment, and the need for recompense. Sometimes the person suffers natural consequences, but we must give up the yearning for vengeance. If the person has hurt us badly, this can be difficult to do, and we need to ask God for help.

11. We fast to nurture our relationship with God, not to impress others. Again, Jesus tells us that when we act to gain favorable opinions of others, we receive our reward from them and not from God.

Developing

14. The group members should consider where they can take a next step toward getting involved in ministering to the body of Christ in your local church. Discuss some of the ministries that your church may offer to people looking to get involved, such as the children's ministry, ushering, or hospitality. Remind everyone that it sometimes takes time and trying several different ministries before finding the one that fits best.

15. Encourage group members to use the *Personal Health Plan* to jot down their next step to serving in ministry, with a plan for how and when they will begin.

Sharing

16. It is important to return to the *Circles of Life* and encourage the group to follow through on their commitments to invite people who need to know Christ more deeply through Christian community. When people are asked why they never go to church they often say, "No one ever invited me." Remind the group that our responsibility is to invite people, but it is the Holy Spirit's responsibility to compel them to come.

17. Take time in this session to extend to your group a call to receive Christ. You can do this using the video segment on the DVD, if you have it, or using the information below.

   If someone in your group is ready to receive Jesus as their Savior now, lead them through the following steps and prayer:

   Express acceptance and belief that Jesus died on the cross for you (1 Cor. 15:2–4).

   Receive his free gift of forgiveness for your sins (Rom. 3:22).

   Begin to live the life God has planned for you and live like you are forgiven (Mark 1:15; Rom. 12:2).

Tell Christ that you want him to lead your life from now on (Rom. 10:9).

You can use the following prayer or pray your own prayer; your heart response toward God is what's important.

Lord, I believe that you sent Jesus to die in my place to pay the price for my sins so I can be forgiven and enter into a relationship with you forever. Forgive me for my sins. I want to live the remainder of my life as you want me to. Fill me with your Spirit to direct me. Amen.

If anyone is not ready to receive Christ at this time, let them know that this is also something they can do at home later if they like. The important thing is to be sure that everyone has had the opportunity to receive Christ personally or have their doubts addressed.

Surrendering

18. It is common for groups to spend most of their time together in the areas of study and fellowship. When this happens, the time for prayer can get squeezed into the remaining minutes of the group. Consider this exercise after your group has met for a few weeks and is ready to go deeper in prayer support.

    Essentially, the *Circle of Prayer* is taking time to spend focused prayer time on each person, or couple, in the group. We suggest you allow each person, or couple, to share for a couple of minutes the needs they are facing. Then have that person stand, sit, or kneel in the middle of the room. The rest of the small group can then join hands around him or her, or place their hands on his or her shoulders if they are comfortable doing that. Group members can then take turns praying for the specific needs shared and ask for God's transforming power to bring change to the situations at hand.

    Since the *Circle of Prayer* takes time, begin doing this exercise this week and continue over the next two sessions so the group doesn't feel pressured to "rush" through the exercise for the sake of time. This time of prayer will bring your group closer together and will remind each of you of God's active presence in your lives. Don't forget to record the individual requests on the *Prayer and Praise Report* to remind you to continue praying for each other between group meetings.

Session Four How to Thrive in Any Economy

Growing

3. We must realize the temporary value of earthly goods and set our minds on accumulating heavenly treasures, which have eternal value. We must put God first, not allowing the worries of this life to distract us from seeking God's kingdom.

4. Jesus emphasizes that material possessions are temporary (we can't take them with us to heaven, and they are vulnerable to rust and decay) and un-

reliable (they easily vanish through theft, stock market drops, or damage). He warns against relying on them for security or status.

5. What we value sets the direction of our hearts, which drives our behavior. If we overvalue money and possessions, we will find it impossible to do the things Jesus tells us to do. We can't hunger for righteousness if we're hungering for money. We can't avoid abusive anger if we're inclined to get enraged when our desire to make more money is thwarted. Greed gets in the way of the generosity Jesus talks about in 6:1–4. Thus, dealing with our attitudes about money is a fundamental aspect of our spiritual growth.

We must guard against placing too high a value on our possessions or wealth. We must not become greedy and hoard our money and material possessions. We must be careful not to trust the security of our future to our material wealth and not let our worldly "treasures" cause self-satisfaction or complacence.

6. We can store up treasures in heaven by investing our financial resources in God's kingdom, seeking to know God more intimately, sharing our faith with others, or serving others in ministry. Anything we do in this life that has eternal value, including praying, fasting, and giving with pure hearts toward God, will store up treasures in heaven. Alternatively, if we value the praise of others, as we talked about in *Session Three*, then we lay up for ourselves treasures on the earth by accumulating their praises.

8. If our spiritual eyes are bad, then we will remain in spiritual darkness, which eventually penetrates our whole being, affecting our actions. This happens as we focus on the things of this world, such as money, material possessions, success, and status and allow them to come first in our lives.

We keep our eyes good by giving attention to what God values, such as the Word of God, worship, prayer, visual reminders of God, and serving him. Devotion to God and focus on his values will bring about spiritual health and wholeness to our lives.

9. The word for *service* here is like as a slave serves a master. Jesus implies that everybody belongs, body and soul, to someone or something. We can't belong completely to God if we're enslaved by our craving for more wealth. If we work toward a raise, promotion, or more possessions, and set our priorities by these things, then we are serving money. We don't have time and energy for both—something ends up compromised. If getting ahead in our career is most important to us, we'll sacrifice time with God in prayer or ministry.

12. To seek God's kingdom first means to fix our eyes on Jesus: to put heavenly concerns above earthly concerns; to make God and his will a priority for our time, energy, and money; to pursue that which expands his kingdom and his purpose above all else. Seeking God's kingdom first will cause our focus to shift from us and our worries to God and his provision. For a typical

person this might involve spending less time on entertainment and more time in prayer. It might mean that a fast-track career takes the back seat to loving and serving one's family and colleagues. Our selfish and fearful hearts will resist when we shift our focus and resources like this! We'll need God's help and the support of fellow Christians.

Developing

14. Point the group to the *Spiritual Gifts Inventory* in the *Appendix*. Read through the spiritual gifts and engage the group in discussion about which gifts they believe they have. Encourage group members to review these further on their own time during the coming week, giving prayerful consideration to each one. We will refer back to this again later in the study.

15. It's time to start thinking about what your group will do when you're finished with this study. Now is the time to ask how many people will be joining you so you can choose a study and have the books available when you meet for the final session of this study.

Sharing

16. This activity provides an opportunity for the group to share Jesus in a very practical way. Discuss this and choose one action step to take as a group. Be certain that everyone understands his or her role in this activity. It might be a good idea to call each person before the next meeting to remind people to bring to the next session what is required of them.

Designate one person to investigate where to donate items in your area. That person can also be responsible for dropping off the items.

Session Five A More Perfect You

Growing

3. Jesus is teaching us to avoid hypocrisy by focusing on our own shortcomings before offering advice or criticism to others. We are to practice discernment, not condemnation, in our estimation of others. We should not worry about our daily needs but depend on God to meet them.

4. The Pharisees often claimed the authority to assess other people's obedience to God and to look down on them based on that judgment. Jesus, however, teaches that we are not to judge contemptuously or hypocritically.

5. Jesus again uses hyperbole to drive home a point. He is not saying it is wrong to help a brother or sister become aware of a fault, but that we must not pass judgment hypocritically. We must deal first with the sins in our own lives, which prevent us from making proper estimation of others. Only as

we develop a self-examining and humble spirit can we rightfully discern another's sin and offer help without condemnation.

6. Again, Jesus uses hyperbole in his use of strong language: "dogs" and "pigs." We should discern other people's character based on their hostile or ungodly actions and relate to them accordingly while maintaining a spirit of love.

   This passage is about spiritual discernment. Giving sacred things to dogs and pearls to pigs is potentially a waste of the resources God has given us. For example, it's not "judgmental" to avoid discussing the gospel with someone who repeatedly attacks it. This is an exercise of discernment, and it can be done while still treating the person with respect. We must utilize all God gives us with care and discernment, as good stewards. Our teaching of others should be in accordance to their spiritual capacity to learn and benefit.

7. Jesus is calling us to persistent and consistent prayer. We should depend upon God in our asking. Transformation of the kind he has been discussing takes time, and we need to resist discouragement and keep praying. This is true of other matters of prayer as well.

9. God delights in giving good gifts to those who ask him. In the same way that parents teach their children by rewarding discipline, persistence, and courtesy, it is through the Father's reward of those who ask, seek, and knock that we learn these same things. Prayer helps us stay focused on the direction of God's will. We need to acknowledge and reject any voice in our hearts that says things like, "God isn't a good parent. He won't give you what you need. Either you take care of yourself, or nobody takes care of you."

10. This is not a promise that we will get everything we selfishly desire, but rather recognition that our heavenly Father wants the best for us, and will always graciously and generously meet our legitimate needs.

11. It is humanly impossible to live out this "Golden Rule" in its intended capacity—not as mere righteous or pious acts, but in true love. It is through the power of the Holy Spirit that we are able to do what Jesus teaches.

Developing

12. If members of the group have committed to spending time alone with God, congratulate them and encourage them to take their commitment one step further and begin journaling. Review *Journaling 101* in the *Appendix* prior to your group time so that you are familiar with what it contains.

Sharing

14. Encourage group members to think about when they are shepherding another person in Christ. This could be simply following through on inviting

someone to church or reaching out to them in Christ's love. Then have everyone answer the question "WHEN are you shepherding another person in Christ?" on the *Personal Health Plan.*

15. It is important to return to the *Circles of Life* often, both to encourage the group to follow through on their commitments as well as to foster growth toward new commitments. Encourage the group this week to consider reaching out to their non-Christian friends, family, and acquaintances. Remind everyone that our responsibility is to share Jesus with others, but it is the Holy Spirit's responsibility to convict souls and bring forth change.

Surrendering

17. Have everyone answer the question "HOW are you surrendering your heart?" on the *Personal Health Plan.*

Session Six False Confidence

Connecting

2. Take a few minutes for group members to share one thing they learned or a commitment they made or renewed during this study. They may also want to share what they enjoyed most about the study and about this group.

   Be prepared to offer some suggested resources for answering questions that may arise from this study. Offer other Scripture that relates to the topics studied. Ask your pastor to suggest some helpful books or articles. Advise group members to schedule a meeting with a pastor to get answers to difficult questions. Whatever you do, don't let anyone leave with unanswered questions or without the resources to find the answers they seek.

Growing

3. Jesus warns against following paths that lead to destruction, he warns of the dangers of false prophets and of false disciples, and he advises us to be careful that we build our lives upon a solid foundation.

4. The broad road of living your life according to your preferences and your culture's habits offers both more comfort and more acceptance from other people. It promises "no questions asked" tolerance and thus is the path of least resistance. The narrow road is the way of persecution and opposition. Only one wholeheartedly dedicated to doing the will of God will knowingly enter through the small gate, because it means enduring suffering.

6. False prophets are those who claim to have been sent by God, but have not been. We can recognize them by the "bad fruit" they bear—their behavior will not line up with the behavior he has been describing in the Sermon on

the Mount. Although he warned us not to be fault-finders (7:1–5), he also warns us to be discerning about leaders. True prophets won't have habits like abusive anger, lust, or breaking their word (5:21–37). They will show love toward those who oppose them (5:38–48). They won't do ministry to show off (6:1–18). They won't be driven by greed (6:19–24). And so on.

7. A true disciple is one who does the will of the Father. This obedience is an expression of genuine saving faith. Someone who claims to believe in Christ but doesn't do what he says doesn't have genuine faith.

8. False disciples are those who on the outside call Jesus "Lord," but in fact they don't let him know them (v. 23). They don't have relationship with him—they aren't surrendered to him. False disciples may know the Bible and even do ministry, but they lack a personal relationship with Jesus which comes through a surrendered heart. This is why the fruit we look for (especially in ourselves) isn't impressive ministry but the kinds of habits Jesus has talked about throughout his sermon.

9. According to this parable, the foundation upon which we build is Jesus's teaching. Building on this foundation involves not simply knowing God's words; it involves putting them into practice. Obedience is not optional. Jesus is not teaching that works produce salvation but that genuine saving faith produces a heart that is obedient to Jesus, which is then demonstrated in our actions. We can compare this to parenting: It is not enough for our children to simply understand our words of discipline; they must demonstrate understanding and change of heart through their actions.

10. When we hit a season of suffering (as everyone does), we will crumble morally if we haven't been building into ourselves habits like consistent, trusting prayer (6:5–13; 7:7–11), true priorities (6:19–34), treating God as our only audience (6:1–18), and so on. If we don't deal with lust, we will be vulnerable to adultery. If we don't deal with selfishness, we will be vulnerable to divorce. Doing what Jesus teaches isn't a nice option for saved people to do or not do, as they prefer. It's an essential part of following the narrow way that leads to life.

Developing

12. Discuss the implication of Jesus's mandate on the lives of believers today to take the gospel to the "ends of the earth." Have each person consider the action steps listed and choose one to begin immediately as a way of doing their part in seeing this accomplished.

13. If you haven't already done so, you'll want to take time to finalize plans for the future of your group. You need to talk about whether you will continue together as a group, who will lead, and where you will meet.

As you discuss the future of your group, talk about how well you achieved the goals you made in the *Small Group Agreement*. Address any changes you'd like to make as you move forward.

Sharing

14. Allow one or two group members to share for a few minutes a testimony about how they helped someone connect in Christian community or shared Jesus with an unbelieving friend or relative.

Surrendering

15. Spend a few minutes devoted solely to sharing praises aloud in simple, one-sentence prayers. Be sure to allow time to share prayer requests. Have one person close the meeting with prayer.

16. Don't forget to close this group time in prayer, praising God for all he accomplished in and through everyone. You can refer back to your *Prayer and Praise Report* for specific praises.

SMALL GROUP ROSTER

Name	Address	Phone	E-mail Address	Team or Role	When/How to Contact You

Pass your book around your group at your first meeting to get every-one's name and contact information.

Name	Address	Phone	E-mail Address	Team or Role	When/How to Contact You

DEEPENING LIFE TOGETHER SERIES

Six **NEW** Studies Now Available!

FRUIT OF THE SPIRIT

JAMES

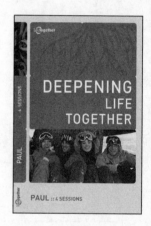

PAUL

PSALMS

RUTH

SERMON ON THE MOUNT

Deepening Life Together is an innovative approach to group Bible study in a DVD format built on the five biblical purposes: **connecting, growing, developing, sharing, and surrendering.**

Each session includes a traditional study guide and a DVD with insightful teaching from trusted scholars and pastors. Included on each DVD are pre-session training videos for leaders and footage from the bestselling *Jesus Film*.

Lifetogether has developed and sold over 2.5 million copies of bestselling, award-winning curriculum for small groups. This DVD series—perfect for small group ministries, Sunday school classes, and Bible study groups—will improve your worship, fellowship, discipleship, evangelism, and ministry.

Studies Available:

ACTS

PRAYING GOD'S WAY

EPHESIANS

PROMISES OF GOD

JOHN

PARABLES

REVELATION

ROMANS

DEEPENING LIFE TOGETHER KIT

The kit includes 8 discussion guides and 8 DVDs: Acts, Romans, John, Ephesians, Revelation, Praying God's Way, Promises of God, and Parables

BakerBooks
a division of Baker Publishing Group
www.BakerBooks.com